Outback in Focus

Outback in Focus

by Jeff Carter

RIGBY LIMITED

Rigby Limited, Adelaide

Sydney, Melbourne, Brisbane, Perth

First published 1968

Copyright 1968 by Jeff Carter

Library of Congress Catalog

Card Number 67-29777

National Library of Australia

Registry Number AUS 67-1710

Designed by Valda Stobie

Printed in Tokyo by Dai Nippon Printing Co. Ltd.

This book is for Mare

This is the Outback I know.

I haven't seen it all. But I have driven, and walked, 250,000 bush miles in the past twelve years. You see and hear and learn a bit in that time.

Apart from a few nights spent in an Alice Springs pub, and the occasional comfort of homestead hospitality or shearing shed accommodation, my camp has always been my swag, under the stars. My pace has been leisurely—a week here, a month there. As a countryman, I know you can't hurry things in the bush. If you want true pictures and facts, you have to wait until they are available. You cannot manufacture them.

The Outback depicted in this book is the dinkum article. It has not been dramatized or glamorized or otherwise abused. The pictures illustrate the land and people over the horizon, as they really are.

I don't regard photography as an art form, although I know it can be, for others. To me the camera is simply an unrivalled reporter's tool. It is an aid to getting the story "properly true" as the Aborigines say. So there are no trick photos in this book— taken with huge telephoto or ultra wide-angle lenses, at odd times, from odd angles, of odd or untypical subjects. To me, such photos are false. They may be art but they don't give a true picture.

So, if ever you do go venturing over the horizon into the Outback, you will see places and people just like those illustrated here. They will appear to you no better, or worse, or different—and then you will know that what I told you was "properly true."

These worn down ranges,
mere ridges on plains of
their own debris,
once towered as high
as the Himalayas

CONTENTS

	PAGE
THE LAND	1
THE PEOPLE	25
THE TOWNS	57
THE ECONOMY	81
THE WILDLIFE	111
TRAVEL	137
HUNTING WITH A CAMERA	151
CAMPING WITHOUT TEARS	164
MOTORING OUTBACK	174

THE LAND

N
Daly
Waters
Broome
Mount
Isa
Carnarvon
Outback
Roma
Nyngan
Port Augusta
Esperance
Hay

My definition of the Outback is that huge tract of dry inland, bigger than Europe and covering more than three-quarters of our continent, which remains beyond the frontiers of agriculture. Most of it is inhospitable to modern man and much of it is antagonistic to man—modern or primitive.

Some parts of the Outback will one day be developed into rural land, through technological know-how and political pressure. The Kimberley area is the most likely example—although for the time being it seems our money could be spent better elsewhere in Australia.

Other pockets of the Outback are also destined to be developed on a limited scale. Towns, if not cities, always spring up around mines and oil wells.

But for the most part, the Outback as we know it today will remain the same for many years to come. It has suffered primitive man's presence for thousands of years, but has actively resisted modern man's efforts to utilize it. The struggle has been going on for almost a century—and the Outback is winning.

The problem of the Outback is water. For the most part, there is none. The highly irregular and extremely low rainfall may briefly fill watercourses and lakes—but these rare bonanzas are quickly sucked up by the hot sun. The annual evaporation rate is almost 8 feet.

Mother Nature, when she was sole custodian of the Outback, handled matters sensibly. She evolved plants to suit the arid climate and grazed few animals on the specialized vegetation. The larger native grazing animals, such as kangaroos, were migratory nibblers of green grass shoots. They did little damage to the larger permanent shrubs and young trees. All wildlife could get along without surface water for long periods.

Primitive man in the Australian Outback followed a similar pattern. He remained small in number, was migratory in habit, and made little impression on the landscape. The harshest areas of sand and gibber he did not penetrate at all. Neither did the specially evolved arid land wildlife.

Out there all was silence. So it remains to this day.

The Outback has often been referred to as the changeless or timeless land. So it used to be. But the times have been changing it at a comparatively rapid rate since modern man's arrival.

On a long term basis, the change has not been for the good of the land or of man.

Before the coming of the white man, the Outback was truly a timeless, changeless land. For thousands, possibly millions of years, change was an almost imperceptible thing. Sandhills in the deserts proper gained ground on one frontier and lost it to stabilizing vegetation on another. Rivers that regularly flowed into lakes at the heart of the continent gradually fell shorter and shorter of their traditional destinations each wet season. Silt brought from watersheds far away filled river beds and caused them to dissipate their waters as floods over the inland plains.

Over thousands of years, the inland lakes became usually dry instead of usually full.

A waterhole on Cooper Creek.
The body of explorer
Robert O'Hara Burke
was found close by

Crumbling, worn down
peaks along the Cooper
near the Queensland-
South Australia border

Some species of vegetation gradually withdrew from certain areas, while others thrived. Trees, shrubs, and grasses advanced here—and retreated there.

Similarly, wildlife populations rose and fell with the seasons. All life in the Inland was modulated like the tides of the ocean—seemingly ever changing, but always the same.

What sort of country is the Australian Outback today? How does it differ from the more hospitable rural land of the eastern seaboard, where most Australians live?

Outback Australia is an old, tired land, probably the oldest in the world. High mountain ranges that once precipitated rain from moisture-laden winds off an inland sea are now low stony ridges. The

sea has gone, and in its place are dusty, sandy plains.

There are no rivers worthy of the name in the entire Outback, except perhaps the Darling, in western New South Wales. All the bold blue lines of the map-makers are generally dry sandy watercourses. The best of them are no more than strings of water-holes. A few of the waterholes are several miles long and are rarely dry, but most of them can be measured in yards and they go dry in the early years of a drought.

The rivers of the Outback flow only after heavy rain, and usually for a few short weeks.

The famous Todd River that passes through Alice Springs makes newspaper headlines if it flows for a day. The Diaman-tina and the Cooper, which both rise in western Queensland, seldom penetrate far into South Australia, although maps show them flowing into Lake Eyre.

The Cooper's poor performance is doubly significant, for it is fed by outback Queens-land's two greatest streams, the Thompson and the Barcoo. The Bulloo River usually peters out before it reaches the north-west corner of New South Wales. The Paroo has a defined channel linking it with the Darling, but the waters of the two streams rarely mix for long. Explorer Charles Sturt tramped across the boldly marked Mulligan River in far west Queensland and didn't even know it!

These are the great names in rivers of the Outback. The size and reliability of the lesser streams can be gauged by comparison. For the most part, they simply do not exist.

Ayers Rock at first seems
insignificant when approached through
the surrounding sand ridges

The climate of the Outback is hot and dry. There is a summer and winter season, but they cannot be compared with the seaboard climatic seasons. In the Outback, the winter tends to be warm and dry, with cold nights. Summer is hot and dry, with hot nights.

There is no set pattern of rainfall, on a yearly basis. Local opinion in some places is that summer storms bring most of the rainfall. This could be true in those locations. But where reliable records have been

The red, glowing domes of Mount Olga, some 20 miles west of Ayers Rock

kept over long periods, there seems to be no definite yearly trend.

The only pattern to outback rainfall seems to be that there tend to be dry periods of up to ten years, followed by two or three high rainfall years. Then adequate rainfall over perhaps eight years, with one or two dry years in between, before the next drought period.

The vegetation of the Outback, in its original state, survived well under these conditions. Trees and shrubs were drought resistant and had no enemies except fire to hinder their growth. Trees like the mulga, corkwood, ghost gum, and desert oak were among the most common species of permanent outback vegetation.

Annual grasses and the smaller flowering shrubs were able to spring from seed to maturity on one or two good falls of rain. The rapidity of their growth gave rise to the myth of the wondrous soil fertility in the Outback. But it was the end product of natural selection, not the richness of the

Desert oaks, west of the Simpson Desert

Traveller's eye view of the Barkly Highway, which links Mount Isa with the Stuart Highway, the 1,000-mile "bitumen" between Alice Springs and Darwin

"Out in the heat of the Never Never that's where the sand dunes dance forever. That's where the dead men lie."
Barcroft Boake

soil, that could convert a dry outback plain, briefly, to a sea of green grass and colourful wild flowers. Vegetation unable to complete its life cycle quickly perished in the arid climate aeons ago. Only the fittest, for the conditions, survived.

Among the fast-growing vegetation that persisted into the white man's time were buckbush, parakeelya, "five minute" grass, and the perennial grasses such as kangaroo, mulga, and Mitchell.

Where plantlife could exist at all in the Australian Outback, there was a good covering of vegetation for such waterless, sunburnt country. After rains or floods, much of the Outback took on an almost parkland mantle. This lasted for several months, occasionally for years.

But inevitably a dry period followed. The grasses and smaller shrubs withered, leaving only their armour-cased seeds in the dust or sand, to wait perhaps years for the next rains. Spinifex, large shrubs, and some trees dried off into a form of suspended animation, alive but apparently dead. What had seemed like a parkland became a silent, forbidding, red-brown place.

These rapid transformations in the appearance of the Outback often confused the early explorers and settlers—sometimes with fatal results.

Explorers pressed on through green, well-watered country toward the heart of the continent; but on the return journey there was no grazing for their horses or water for their canteens. Pioneer settlers took up what appeared to be good grazing country and watched their herds grow; but a few years later their sheep and cattle were dead of starvation or bogged in drying waterholes.

This sort of outback country climate prevails throughout most of western Queensland and New South Wales, the north-eastern quarter of South Australia, and around Alice Springs. I have not been to Western Australia, but from my reading it seems that similar country and climate

The colours of the Centre.
Tourists in the Amphitheatre,
south-west of Alice Springs

**Drift sand building
on semi-poisonous shrubs,
the only surviving vegetation
on this over-grazed land**

**Rain can block outback
"roads" for weeks. This is a
typical creek crossing in
Queensland's Channel Country**

exist west of a line drawn from Esperance to Port Hedland (excluding the better rural lands in the south-west corner).

The Top End of the Northern Territory, the adjacent Kimberley region, and Queensland's Cape York area, while classed as "Outback" by virtue of remoteness, are monsoon-affected, potential agricultural areas—and outside the scope of this book.

The remainder of what I call the Outback is harsh, inhospitable land, antagonistic to any form of extensive and permanent usage by man. The bastions of this country are our deserts proper: the Arunta (Simpson) Desert, Sturt's Stony Desert, the Great Victoria Desert, the Gibson Desert, the Great Sandy Desert, and the Tanami Desert.

Despite the grandiose schemes of the lunatic fringe of outback "experts," our deserts won't flow with milk and honey within the foreseeable future. No plough will furrow the red dunes; no crops will flourish on the claypans; no herds will graze where now there are gibbers.

Modern man has laid claim to these deserts for more than a century, but so far has kept out of them. The only habitations in them are government weather stations and oil or mineral prospecting camps. Apart from the possibility of a few small oil or mining towns, if strikes are made, our deserts proper are likely to remain for ever empty of permanent settlers.

But deserts aren't defined by fences or other clear lines of demarcation. They usually lie at the heart of much larger areas of arid or semi-arid marginal lands. Into

This man-made dam in northern South Australia has made it possible for sheep and cattle to graze surrounding country bare

Overleaf:
Motoring on the Dajarra Road, south of Mount Isa

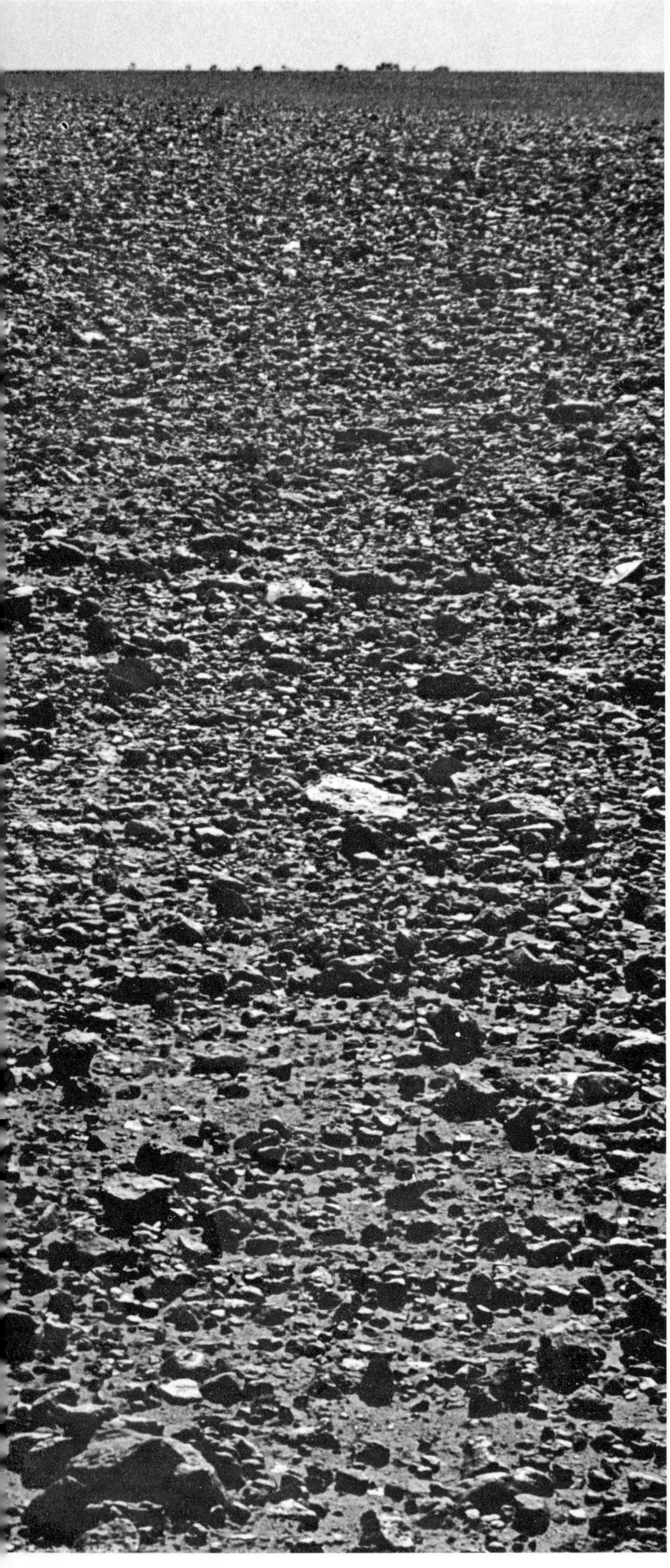

Left:
Man cannot be blamed for this dismal scene in Sturt's Stony Desert, which the explorer described as "a landscape which never changed, but for the worse . . ."

Right:
Deterioration of this centralian landscape is due to 70 years of continuous grazing, not drought

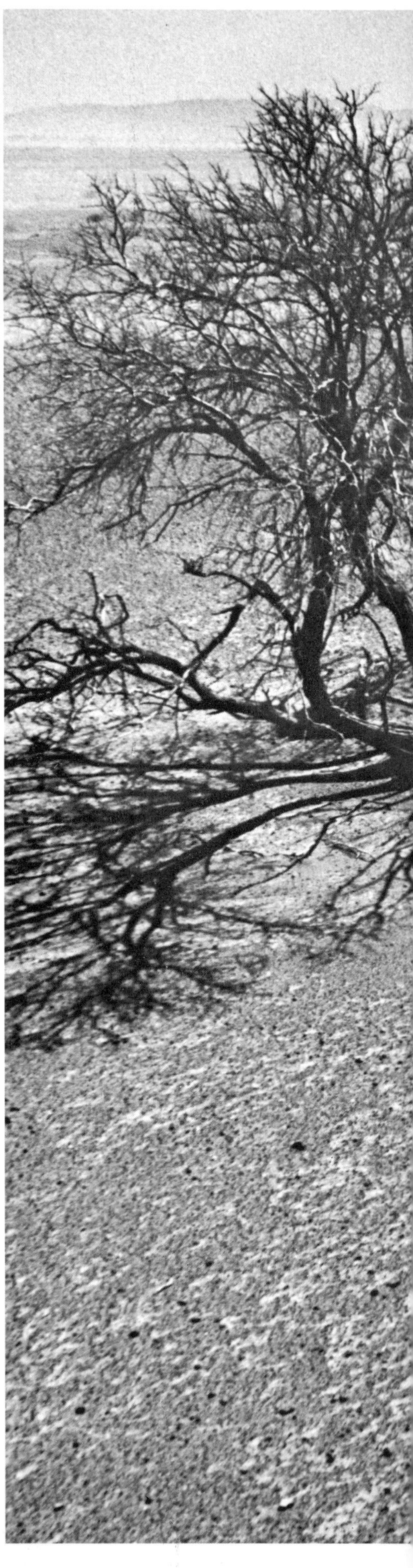

these they encroach from time to time, and then recede, according to the seasons.

Man has kept out of the deserts, but for the last hundred years he has battled grimly to occupy and use the marginal country surrounding them. Pioneer graziers reached the Outback proper in the 1850s. They tried to make use of it by grazing sheep and cattle on vegetation that had never supported anything more than an occasional passing mob of nibbling kangaroos.

In the best of the marginal lands, their flocks and herds did well for a time. Other settlers pushed out further, in good seasons penetrating unwittingly almost to the deserts proper.

Once they were acclimatized to it, the sheep and cattle thrived on the saltbush, grasses, and shrubs of the dry Outback. They ate even the leaves of the trees.

But the good years passed and the inevitable drought followed. The grasses died, the bushes browned off, the trees failed to produce fresh, edible leaves. Cattle and sheep died in thousands. Homesteads were abandoned.

Then good seasons came again, and with them another wave of optimistic settlers. Cattle and sheep populations grew. So did the number of rabbits, which were then invading the Outback in teeming millions.

The previous cycle was repeated. For a time things went well. Some men grew rich. Then drought came again and there was

Below:
Emus flee toward a shimmering mirage across a well-clothed plain east of Bourke, New South Wales

**Ayers Rock from a sand
dune crest beside the
Mount Olga road**

another retreat. But good seasons eventually followed and the settlers came back with their cattle and sheep.

By then it had been discovered there was good stock-drinking water far beneath the ground. Artesian and sub-artesian bores made it possible for the herds and flocks to range over more and more of the Outback. Where once a man's sheep and cattle grazed over only a few thousand of his million acres, through lack of natural waterholes, now the livestock ranged over every square yard of it.

Vegetation that had previously been beyond the limits of grazing was chewed down by the soaring numbers of sheep and cattle. On many heavily stocked properties, young grass brought up by the rain was eaten down before it could leave seed for a further crop.

And still the rabbits multiplied.

Drought came again and this time seemed worse than ever. Good times followed, but they seemed not quite so good. Fewer of the edible grasses and shrubs reappeared. Instead, it looked as if the less palatable vegetation was on the increase.

In some places, where once there had been plenty, nothing much grew at all. The earth, eaten naked and churned up by cloven hooves, had dried to powder and blown away in the last drought. Land that once had run a sheep to every ten acres now only supported one on twenty acres.

In the next drought, natural waterholes filled with sand and disappeared for ever. The dust of the Outback darkened cities as far away as Sydney. When the rains eventually came, it took forty acres to support one sheep.

This gradual deterioration of the outback landscape is still going on today. At first the change was almost imperceptible, but the rate is accelerating with each drought.

21

Land that was once marginal but with good vegetation cover is now bare. A Royal Commission on outback New South Wales commented on the possibility of this as early as 1890. Where once grass grew after rain there are now bare claypans. Fences and buildings lie buried under sand. Scores of homesteads are now abandoned ruins. Once thriving settlements are today empty ghost towns. Surviving towns offer little but memories of their hey-days. Each year it takes a few more acres to graze each sheep, more square miles to graze the same number of cattle.

Anyone who doubts these facts need only talk to the botanists, zoologists, and geographers who have made studies of the Outback. Their findings are all in print. So are the statistics on grazing rates. The ruined homesteads, empty towns, and buried fences are there for anyone to see.

I think our outback lands cannot much longer support our traditional form of utilization. By and large, the grazing of our marginal lands will have to stop, or be drastically reduced and strictly controlled.

Fortunately, a new era is dawning in the Australian Outback—that of tourism. Already outstripping grazing as a money earner in the heart of Australia, it represents a safe form of land utilization. I sincerely believe it is the only way outback Australia can avoid becoming the nation's dead heart.

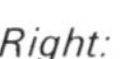

Right:
Tourists have but recently descended on the Outback, but do less damage to the landscape than livestock, and produce higher returns

Left:
Sub-artesian water, pumped to the surface by windmills, allowed sheep and cattle to be loosed on country meant for kangaroos

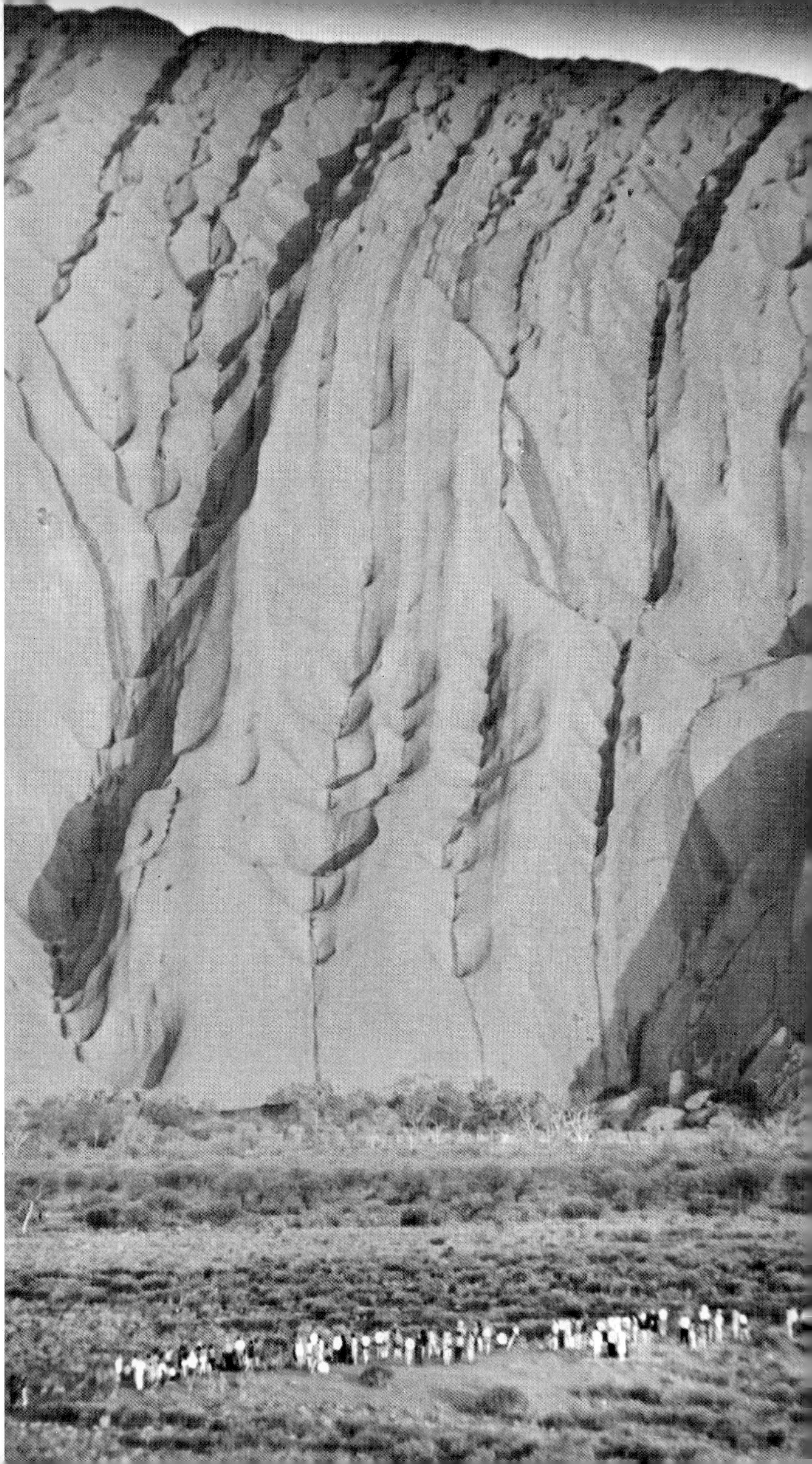

THE PEOPLE

The people of the Outback, black or white, have always lived off the land, in the true sense of the phrase.

Primitive nomadic Aborigines hunted over the landscape for thousands of years. They didn't till the soil or shepherd flocks. They just plucked nature's crops, and moved on. The men hunted kangaroos, emus, lizards, and other small game. The women collected seeds, berries, edible insects, bush honey, and anything else provided by nature that could be eaten.

When tucker got short in one area, they moved on to another, within their own tribal territory. They took what they needed from the country and put nothing into it, save their bones. It was a parasitic form of existence, but as the Aborigines were few in number, they did little harm to the land.

Since his coming, the white man has also lived off the land. The history of our settlement of the Outback is one of taking. We have put nothing back into the land. So we are no better than the black man, in this respect.

In fact, we are a whole lot worse. The Aborigine took from the land only what he needed to survive. Modern man has taken far more, for profit rather than to meet his needs.

First he took the land forcibly from the Aborigines. Then he shot and poisoned all those he didn't require as underpaid workers. Next he introduced hordes of insatiable grazing animals to eat the country bare. True, he built some dams and fences, but these were simply aids to allow him to take more out of the country.

Modern man's existence in the Outback has been every bit as parasitic as the Aborigine's. But where the Aborigine took little, we have taken much—too much.

We have even taken the wildlife from the landscape, at least all we could get our hands on, largely for profit. The bigger animals have been harvested for their fur and flesh, emus for their feathers—even their eggs were exported as curios. Practically every other creature, furred or feathered, big enough to get in the sights of a rifle, has been indiscriminately slaughtered, for the pot, for sport, or in the name of pest eradication.

That is the black side of white settlement of the Australian Outback. Is there a brighter chapter?

Yes, I know there is, but it is too early yet to be written. Modern man's best works in the Outback are far from completed—in some fields they have scarcely begun.

I am the first to admit that it is easy to point up the mistakes of the past and highlight the errors of the many, while overlooking the good works of the few. A percentage of outback dwellers have always

Friendly, but doubtful now,
this youngster's attitude to
white men will almost
inevitably harden into
active dislike. The onus is
squarely on the white
majority to win
the respect and trust
of the black minority

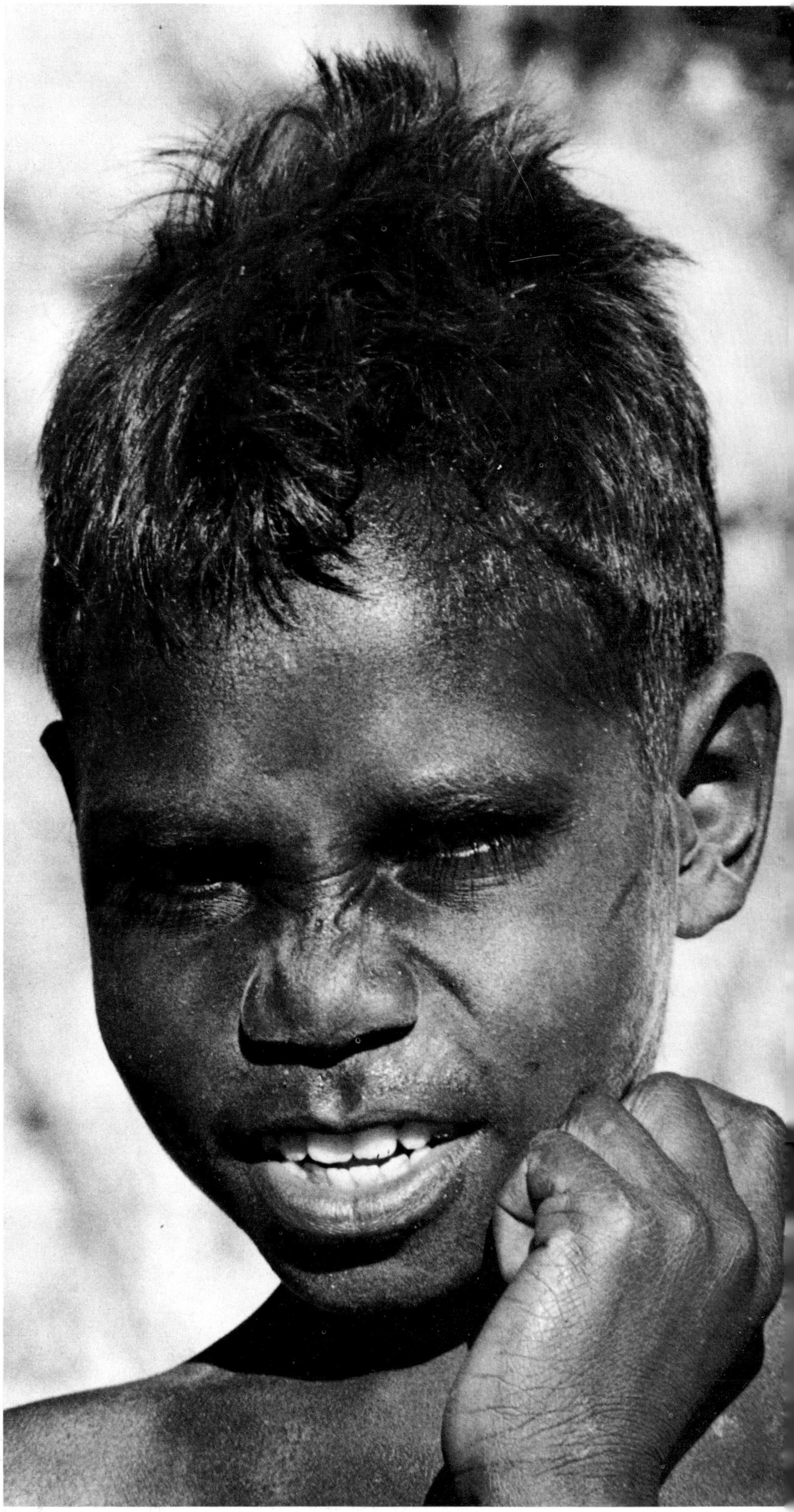

Left:
This Wailbri
tribesman is amongst
the last generation
of Aborigines
still capable
of a nomadic life

Centre:
This man could still live
in the bush, too,
but looks to the
ways of the white man
for a better life

Right:
This Alice Springs
policeman works as
a white man, but is
not paid as a
white man or
treated like one

refused to join in the rape of the land, the slaughter of the wildlife, and the degradation of the Aborigines. Some of them have been squatters claiming dominion over thousands of square miles of country.

Others have been humble station hands or prospectors whose only claim on the Outback has been a few acres staked out on a mining lease. Some have been drovers, or shearers, or tank sinkers, publicans, men of God, or just plain rolling stones. In every group there have been individuals any Australian would be proud to know.

John Flynn, Alfred Traeger, Bill Harney, and D. W. McLeod are shining examples.

And there is much that is good in the character of modern Australians that owes its origins to the outback way of life. Initiative, self-reliance, independence, the unique talent for improvisation—these national traits were all born or at least fine-honed in the bush.

Collectively, the outback grazier is something of a blight on the land, but individually he is nearly always a good bloke. I like most of the squatters I know, although

I often knock them as a group.

Some are enlightened men who are trying to correct the errors of the past by more sensible land usage. In my opinion, the dice are now loaded heavily against them—and their efforts would be better spent in other directions—perhaps in running tourists instead of cattle or sheep.

Many outback graziers of today are just as blind and stubborn in refusing to accept the evidence of their own eyes as their grandfathers were. They will go down with their homesteads beneath the shifting sands, like the pioneers who once lived in today's ruins and ghost towns. But it does no good to criticize individuals. When you are born and bred in one place and know no other way of life, you cannot be too severely blamed for refusing to give it up.

It is surely the Government's responsibility to formulate an enlightened policy of outback land usage, even if this involves resettling some people elsewhere. It would be cheaper in the long run than the present subsidizing of ruinous grazing enterprises—through road and railway and stock route

Aluminium tropical huts like this one are made available to selected Aboriginal families on government settlements. About one per cent of Aborigines on settlements live in such homes

construction and maintenance, freight concessions, costly administration, tax exemptions, and so on.

But there are other people in the Outback besides graziers. Who are they?

There are the Aborigines, for a start—and their poor relations, the half-castes. Throughout much of the Outback, these groups form a large section of the population.

In the Northern Territory, for example, there are 23,000 full-blood Aborigines, plus 2,300 half-castes, compared with 27,000 Europeans (of which 15,000 are in Darwin). In Queensland, the combined underprivileged population, black, brown, and brindle, is over 20,000. Many of these people live in the Outback, outnumbering whites on most stations and smaller settlements. The situation is no doubt similar in outback Western Australia, where the combined black and brown population is around 20,000.

There are few full-blood Aborigines in outback New South Wales today—perhaps 1,000—but the state's half-caste population is around 13,200, many of whom live in the bush. The casual visitor to towns like Wanaaring or Tibooburra doesn't have to be a demographer to gauge what shade of citizen is in the majority.

What is the status of this large segment of the Australian outback population? It should be good, for in many of the furthest out places, particularly in the Northern Territory and Queensland, the coloured population provides the major work force.

Unfortunately the black, brown, and

"creamy" people of the Outback are as downtrodden and underprivileged as ever.

There are exceptions, but by and large, if you are Aboriginal or half-caste in the Outback, your lot is roughly this: you work for practically nothing, you live in a humpy well away from the homestead, or out of town, you keep out of most pubs and certain shops—and in the presence of any white man, it is prudent to be humble.

The days when squatters on lonely stations could with impunity beat or even kill Aboriginal or half-caste employees are over—but only just.

The status of these people is summed up in this anecdote concerning an Alice Springs policeman. I had called several times at the police station, asking for an Aboriginal tracker by name. He had been particularly mentioned in a National Geographic Magazine story I had been commissioned to illustrate. Each day I called at the police station, the man I wanted was out and the policeman said there was another "one" out the back who would do just as well. But I wanted the particular man mentioned by name in the story.

On my fourth visit, the policeman became a little exasperated and said: "What's the matter with you? They're all black, aren't they?"

Legislation is trying to improve the lot of coloured people, but until there is a change of heart among the white population of the Outback, the new laws are scarcely worth the paper they are written on.

Everything is comparative, of course. To the eyes of a city dweller, the lot of even the white outback citizen is arduous and generally uninviting. Except in a handful of the flashest homesteads a lot of the amenities of city life are missing.

Electricity is almost unknown, apart from household lighting plants, so there are no electric stoves, radiators, refrigerators, or washing machines in most homes. The only automatic hot and cold water is the hot water of summer and the cold water of winter. When cooking has to be done or hot water is required, a fire has to be lit.

A fire means wood—and this in turn means someone has to get busy with chain saw and axe, regularly.

When stores are needed, it may be a 50 or 100 mile return trip to get them. Fresh bread and meat don't arrive on the doorstep. Outback dwellers have to bake the first and kill the second. Fresh milk is almost unknown.

There are no flushing toilets or regular

garbage collections. Someone has to dig holes each week. And so it goes on.

The average outback dwelling is a crude structure compared with most suburban homes. Many are of corrugated iron, only partly lined, although the outback winter is colder and the summer hotter than anything city dwellers know. There is no television at night, or pub down the road. Outside the tiny towns, which are few and far between, there are no friendly neighbourhood stores for recreational gossiping.

There is more to the 50 or 100 mile trip to town than meets the eye. Most roads in the Outback are what bitumen-soft city dwellers would term impassable tracks. If it

Left:
**This old Murray cod
fisherman, dead now,
was among the last of
his trade. Today
the river produces chiefly
redfin, few cod**

Right:
**Bullock drivers are among
the ranks of bush workers who
have faded from the
outback scene. A few survive**

rains on the way, a vehicle is likely to be bogged for a day or two, or cut off on the return journey by a flooded creek.

When this happens, all mum and the kids back at the homestead can do is wait—and tighten their belts if necessary. Equally long delays can be experienced if the man of the house gets trapped in the town pub by old cronies. Then he may arrive back at the homestead a week late and with only half the supplies he meant to get.

Even when the trip is not impaired by liquid of any sort, the patient cook may find her (or his) long-awaited supplies badly scrambled on arrival.

Outback roads are rough and dusty. It is common for eggs, jars, and crockery to be broken, the butter melted, treacle or sugar spilled, and for dust to have found its way into everything.

Outback life is synonymous with outdoor life. The most common forms of outback life are flies and ants. These, plus the heat, make work doubly arduous. Which is why so little gets done at times.

But when conditions are right, outback toilers perform some prodigious feats and take a pride in their work that is almost unknown to city factory and office workers.

The proudest outback worker is the drover, but his work is no bed of roses. He rarely enjoys even the rude shelter of an outback homestead. His job occupies him seven days a week and he works from starlight to starlight each day, and puts in a few hours' watch at night, too, if he is travelling cattle.

But he likes it.

Aboriginal women making soap at Banka Banka Station, in the Northern Territory. Conditions for Aborigines on this station managed by a widow, are comparatively good . . . but few white people would willingly swop places with a black station worker, male or female

Most other outback workers are the same—they like the life. Most of them are born and bred on the backblocks, but usually they have had one "go" at the city, and disliked it. "Too flamin' much hurry-up down there for me," is the commonest complaint. To which is often added: "They're all flyin' round like blue-arsed flies in a pickle bottle and gettin' nowhere. . . ."

So the drover stays out on the track in all weathers, the squatter is happy to be king, even in the most humble castle, and the station hands are satisfied with their unlined corrugated iron men's quarters.

What of the others—the fencing contractors, the tank sinkers, the water borers, the dingo trappers, the rabbit and kangaroo shooters, the shearers, the truck drivers, the bush pilots, the shop-keepers and publicans?

They are of the same mind as the graziers and the drovers, who are the backbone of the Outback. They like the place and the life—with all its rigours.

A liking for adventure, of a sort, keeps some men in the backblocks. The frontier era hasn't ended yet in the Outback—not by a long chalk. There are still hard-bitten men who live by the gun.

They don't wear side-arms and duel in the sun at high noon. Today's professional gunmen are still frontiersmen of a sort. They are hunters, harvesting the flesh and fur of the kangaroo, the rabbit, and the wild goat. Theirs is a tough, uncertain way of life, with perhaps an element of adventure to it.

If you want
chops, mutton, or
lamb's fry in the Outback,
first kill your sheep . . .

. . . and a cool drink
doesn't come out of the
fridge or a bar room tap, but
from the traditional
bushman's waterbag

Bored or restless city men shouldn't dream of going outback to shoot their way to fame and fortune. There's little romance in professional shooting. It is largely hard work. Loneliness, heat, flies, dust storms, freezing winter winds, and constant physical discomfort are part of the job. Working with animals, guns, and knives is dangerous enough, and isolation makes it doubly so, if there is an accident. A wounded man can die with his boots on before help comes.

When times are good, a kangaroo or rabbit shooter can earn big money, for perhaps five months of the year. While targets are plentiful and prices high, he may gross $200 a week. But with costs deducted and earnings averaged over a year, the picture is not so rosy.

When times are tough, which they often are, professional hunters turn to pest destruction, shooting a variety of animals for their scalps: dingoes, brumbies, and sometimes camels. No one ever became rich doing this.

Full-time professional kangaroo and

There is a myth that
Aborigines are slow learners
and slow workers.
But they are no slower
than a white man would be if he
were paid only $10 or less
for a full week's work

The most unlikely outback
characters have a story to tell.
This old man, poling his boat
along the Murray, recalled
the burning of the paddle-steamer
Rodney, during the shearers'
strike of the 1890s

A centre cattleman
scans the sky
for rain that may
still be years away

A young drover's shepherd
of western New South Wales has
already the sun-creased eyes
of his father's trade

A professional rodeo rider
in outback Queensland
observes the opposition with
studied nonchalance

rabbit shooters can operate profitably only when their quarry is present in large numbers. Most kangaroo shooting is done inside the great dingo-proof fence which runs across South Australia, New South Wales, and Queensland.

Protected from their natural enemy the dingo, kangaroos have thrived inside their giant paddock since the coming of the white man. The presence of graziers' bores has enabled them to range over wider tracts of land. In places, the presence of sheep has increased the kangaroo population. For example scientific investigation in Western Australia reveals that sheep eat out food the 'roos don't like and make way for plants they relish. Also, the 'roos don't like tough old grass and shrubs, but they love the fresh green shoots that sprout after the less fussy sheep have chewed down the old plants.

It is likely that the kangaroo population has been increasing inside the protection of the dingo fence during the past fifty years, despite constant shooting.

Outside the fence, where shooters rarely operate, the kangaroo population is notably sparser than it is inside. However, since kangaroo meat became popular as pet food in 1959, the shooting rate has greatly increased. Recent aerial surveys indicate that numbers are dwindling to a perhaps dangerous low.

In view of this, I think professional shooting of kangaroos should be halted until scientists complete various field studies now in progress. Until this work is finished, no one really knows what he is talking about when he gets on to kangaroos in the Outback.

Although the kangaroo is our national animal, our ignorance about the creatures

**Shearing is one of the few
really well-paid trades in the Outback,
and conditions are good. But the
work is hard and pay and conditions
hard won. Ask any squatter**

**Boundary riding is a common outback
occupation, but this man's job is unusual.
He rides (and repairs) a section
of the longest fence in the world . . .
the 6,000-mile Wild Dog Fence**

is monumental, as any discussion on their breeding, feeding, or migratory habits will disclose. Contradictory statements come thick and fast. There are still plenty of adherents to the notion that the young kangaroo is "born on the teat."

Conservationists say a kangaroo eats less than a sheep. Graziers maintain a kangaroo eats as much as five sheep. Scientists point out that they eat different foods, so the argument is futile anyway.

On the other hand, no one complains about professional rabbit shooters. Their trade is free of controversy. They operate largely outside the dingo fence, in the lonely sandhill country of South Australia and adjacent south-west Queensland. Shooting methods are the same as for kangaroos. Four-wheel-drive vehicles are used at night. Telescopic sights are fitted on .22 rimfire rifles, as all rabbits have to be shot in the head. The normal vehicle headlights are used, because powerful spotlights frighten the rabbits. The range is usually only 70 feet.

A good shooting average is ten pairs an hour. The shooter stops every hour and guts his rabbits, hanging them in pairs on poles across the back of his vehicle. Good shooters in prolific areas tally from fifty to a hundred pairs nightly.

Four shooting nights a week is considered satisfactory. Bad weather, mechanical breakdowns, or the presence of dingoes stop operations on the other nights.

The rabbits have to be delivered to mobile chillers before sunrise each day. This may mean a drive of 40 miles. Average

A governess
supervises correspondence
lessons on an outback
station veranda.
School of the Air
classes supplement but
do not replace
correspondence courses

price paid at the chiller is around 40 cents a pair. Out of this have to come nightly operating costs of at least $10.

Although the money can be good at times, professional rabbit shooting isn't everyone's cup of tea. Water is always scarce, even washing water, unless camp happens to be near an artesian bore. Drums of drinking water are carted up to 200 miles from towns like Broken Hill or Tibooburra.

In some parts of the Outback, domestic goats gone wild are a serious pest. They ring-bark young trees and devour grass and shrubs favoured by sheep. Previously always shot haphazardly as pests, they are now being harvested on an organized scale in some places by professional shooters for sale as pets' meat.

Wild horses (brumbies) are regarded as vermin for almost the same reasons as goats are. A brumby shooter may be paid a wage or so much a head. He also makes a bit extra by selling hair from the manes and tails of the horses he shoots. (It is still used by the medical profession for stitching in certain operations.)

Dingo shooting is only a sideline among professional hunters. The bounty is less than $1 a head where they are plentiful. But inside the fence, where they are rare, it goes as high as $4. The idea, of course, is to do your shooting outside the fence and collect your bounties on the inside.

Not all outback dwellers are born and bred in the bush. There are New Australians among them and men from the cities and large rural towns. A few may be

This Irish-born girl
was cook at the Betoota hotel
in far west Queensland
last time I called

The new invaders
of the Outback . . .
engineers in hard hats . . . head
the task forces of mining
and other companies

hiding from the police, or their wives, or the taxation commissioner, but most have fetched up in the backblocks because it is the life they like best.

There is something about country with few fences or visible restrictions of any kind that appeals to some people. It allows them to develop what individuality they have and maintain an independence of spirit that would be put down and crushed in the bustling cities.

For this form of freedom they are prepared to put up with flies, heat, dust, isolation, poor wages, monotonous food, and a hard bed. In return, they escape the oblivion and loneliness of the city.

In recent years, a new kind of people have come to the Australian Outback. The first of them were prospectors, but very different from the traditional fossicker with his pick, shovel, and dry blower. They hovered over the land in helicopters,

or rolled across once impassable country in strange new machines.

Their tools were aerial cameras and seismographs and drilling rigs.

Gold was the last thing they thought of. They searched for other minerals and valuable substances locked beneath the earth's surface. They found them: uranium, manganese, bauxite, phosphates, natural gas, and oil.

Now the first mines are working and oil is beginning to flow.

Modern machines, the task force of unlimited capital, are establishing settlements, roads, and other facilities with unprecedented speed. But this form of development, dotted here and there in isolated corners, will bring little change to the Outback in general.

Most of the new products of the Outback are being taken away in their crude form, to be processed elsewhere—mostly over-

Left:
Yarning round the campfire is the chief form of daily recreation for drovers on the track

Right:
Drovers are early to bed and early to rise . . . so it saves time and trouble if you sleep with your boots (and spurs) on

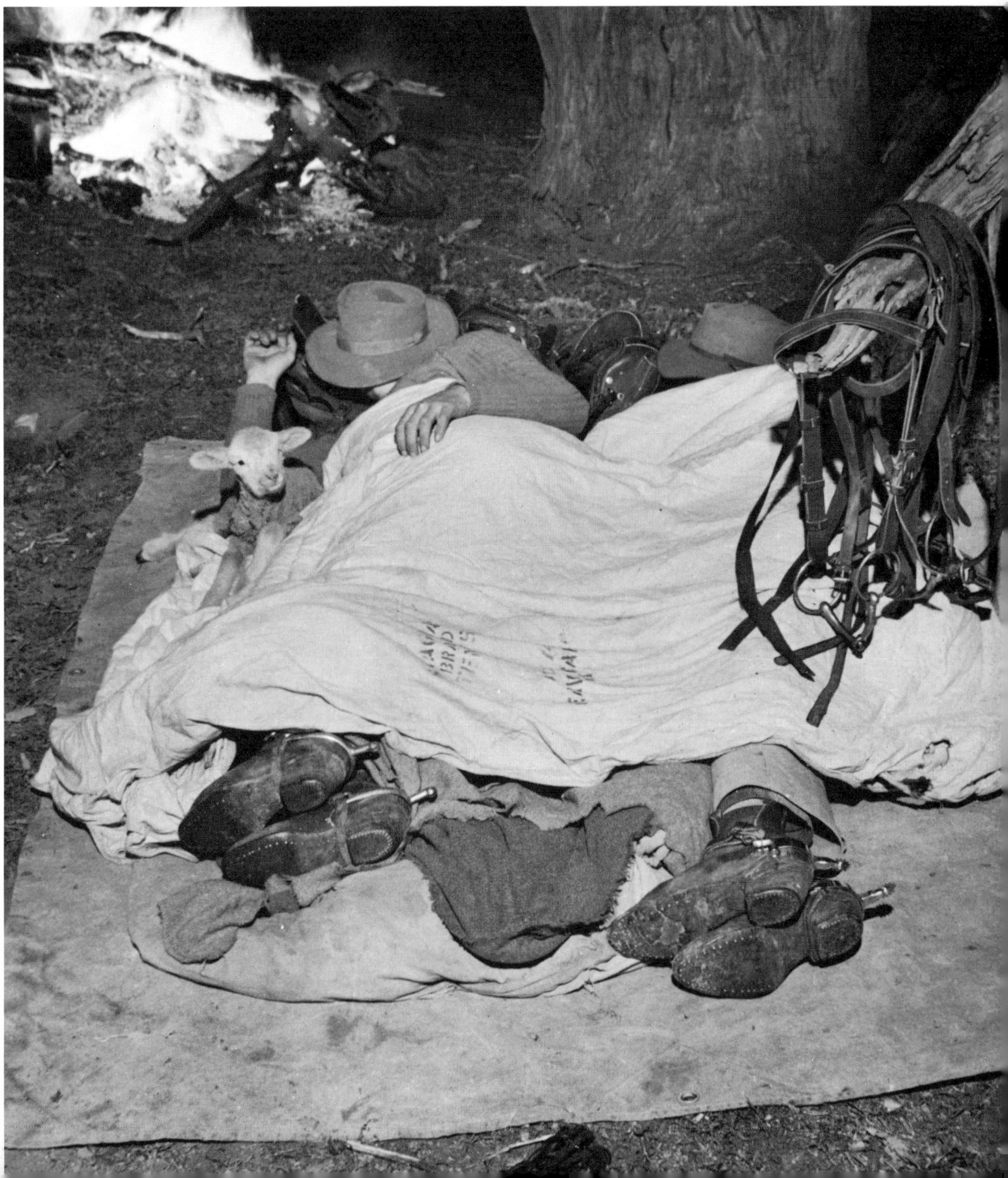

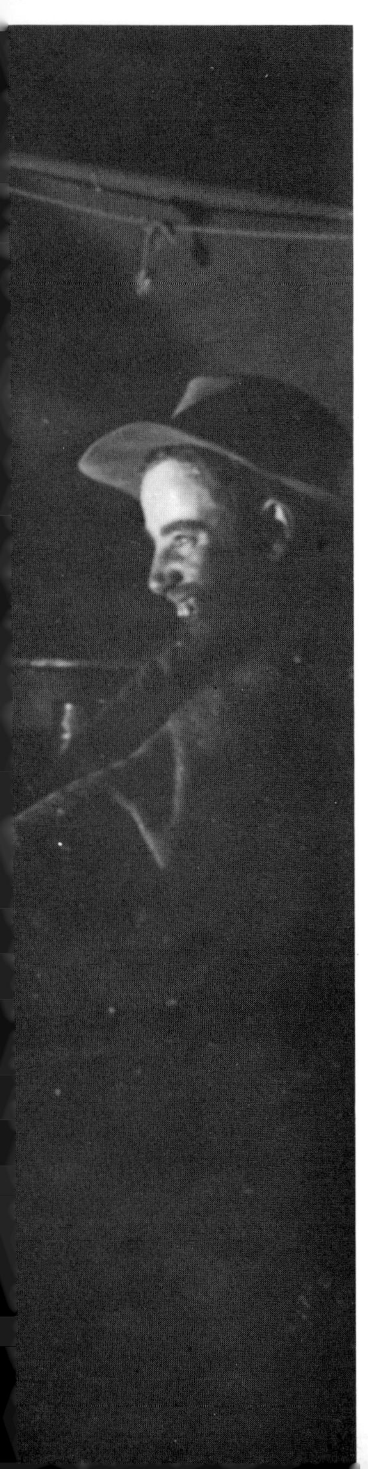

seas. The newcomers, like the oldtimers, are putting little into the Outback, except holes in the ground. The traffic is all one way—out.

The men in the hard hats with the strange accents are living off the land, like the graziers and trappers before them, and the Aborigines before them. Thus nothing in the Outback really changes. It all seems new and progressive at first, but in reality it is the same old pattern in the same old changeless, timeless land.

The only places where there is real likelihood of development are the more favoured pockets of the Outback, such as the Kimberleys and the Gulf Country. Government scientific bodies, notably the C.S.I.R.O., have been studying these areas for years. They have produced pilot schemes for more efficient beef raising enterprises and shown that agriculture is feasible, when the time is ripe.

But these areas are really outside the scope of this book, which deals with the arid and semi-arid Outback, where agriculture beyond market-garden scale is out of the question in the foreseeable future.

The only big and far-reaching changes that will alter the outback way of life in general will take place when graziers run kangaroos and tourists instead of sheep and cattle—and when black, brown, and cream-skinned people are encouraged to live like human beings.

Left:
**This man has an unusual
job in the Outback . . .
fireman on a tramway!
The "tramway" is really a railway,
linking Broken Hill with
South Australia. Like most
outback railways, it was
completed long before
Federation in 1901**

Right:
**Although he now loses
some jobs to road trains, the
traditional drover will
be a familiar figure
on the outback skyline for
many years to come**

THE TOWNS

Acres of bottles and
crumbling stone walls are all
that remain of the historic
town of Innamincka.
Once there was a hospital
and near by, a cemetery where
men were buried between sheets
of corrugated iron.
There was no wood available
for coffin building

Previous page:
The ruins of Ryan's Well
homestead, north of
Alice Springs on what is
now the Stuart Highway

Many of the Outback's towns and settlements are gone, or going. Man has retreated from the arid backblocks more than he has advanced into them during the last half a century.

Arltunga is gone; Innamincka is gone; Milparinka is gone; Thackaringa, Mount Gipps, Silverton, and Waukaringa are gone. Places like Marree, Oodnadatta, Birdsville, Bedourie, Eulo, Hungerford, Halls Creek, Wanaaring, and a score of others hang on, not quite ghost towns yet, but mere shadows of their former selves. Birdsville once had three pubs—a couple of years back, half the one surviving establishment, built of stone and lime mortar, literally fell down.

Some places, still prominently marked on the map, were scarcely ever really there at all, as fully fledged towns. Take Betoota for example—one building, a pub. Nothing else. There are plenty of other examples: Barringun, Windorah, Beltana, Newcastle Waters. Try to find Gilgunnia, which is supposed to be in central New South Wales, scarcely in the real Outback at all. Try to buy anything more than beer or petrol in that legendary town of Booligal.

At scores of map-marked "towns" you can usually buy beer or petrol, seldom both, and frequently neither. A meal is almost out of the question.

Apart from Alice Springs, the capital city of the Outback, which is thriving as a result of the tourism boom, almost every town in the dry backblocks' country is dying. The exceptions are the mining towns such as Broken Hill, Mount Isa,

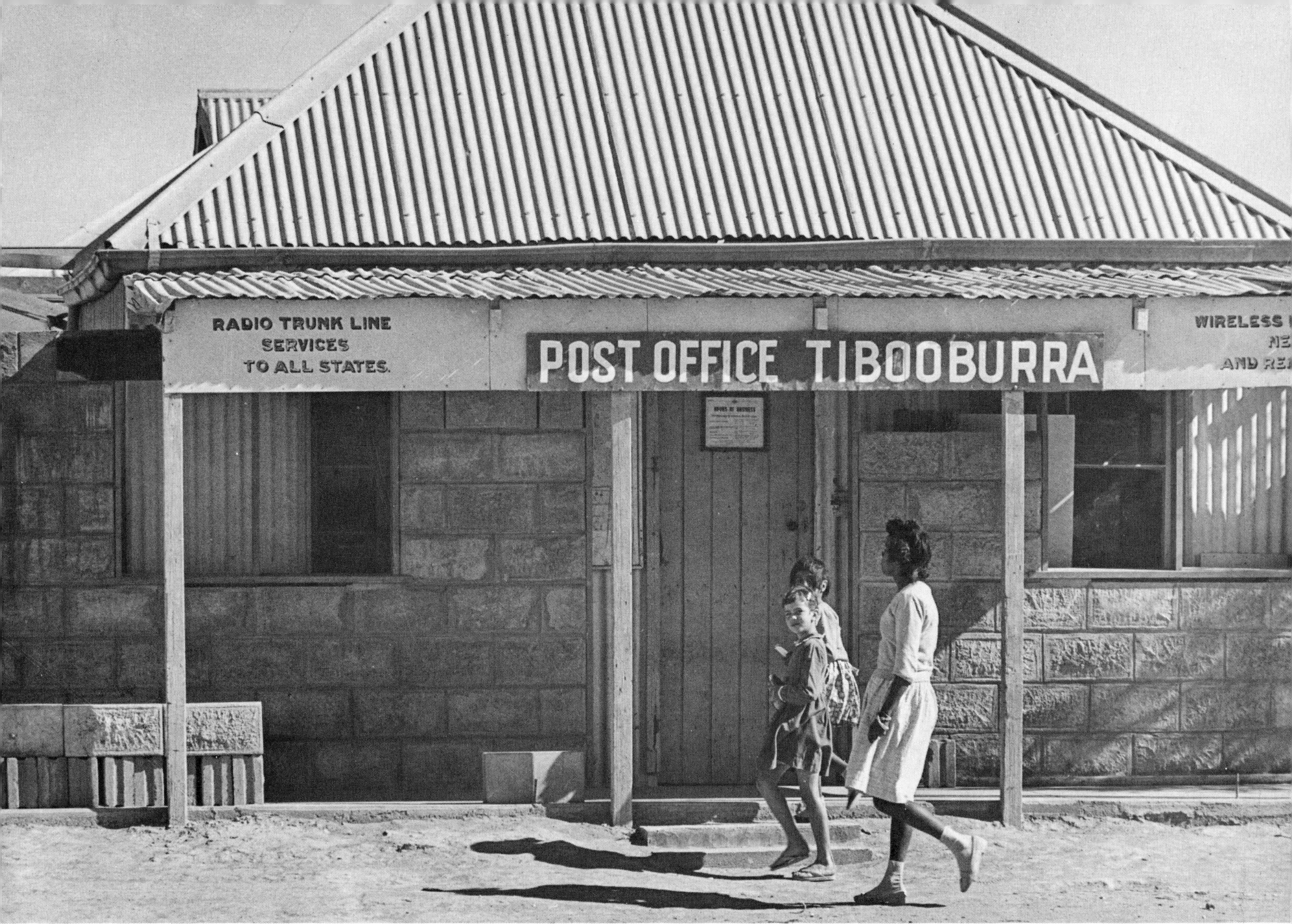

Tennant Creek, Kalgoorlie, and Leigh Creek. A handful of smaller settlements are just poking along. The best example I know in this category is Tibooburra, in far north-west New South Wales.

On the perimeter of the Outback proper, the substantial big towns are holding their own, but (oil or mineral strikes aside) they are scarcely booming. This group includes Winton, Longreach, Charleville, Cunnamulla, Bourke, Cobar, Hillston, Hay, and Balranald. The last mentioned are saltbush communities, owing much of their prosperity to the ability of saltbush to withstand constant grazing by sheep. Recent botanical surveys indicate that even saltbush is not indestructible.

It is a fair bet that most of the declining smaller towns will continue to shrink until they become invisible—unless someone strikes oil or mineral wealth near by. These are the places where even now there is only a pub and perhaps a general store. A few, like Wanaaring in far western New South Wales, boast a post office and garage as well.

Many of these places have been reduced to a pub and nothing more. The pub is usually the last establishment to go. It was thus at Innamincka, now a ghost town, and it is thus at Birdsville.

In such places the pub often doubles as the town store, selling groceries from a disused bar room or parlour. Deliveries of goods arrive rather uncertainly via long and dusty roads. Garden-fresh vegetables and fruit or farm-fresh eggs are hard to come by. Fresh meat is unprocurable—everyone kills his own. The main stock in trade comprises tinned goods, travel-weary potatoes, and onions on occasion and sometimes bread.

To purchase these items is rarely a simple matter of breasting a counter and making a selection from the shelves. Usually the publican has to be approached in the bar and eventually he or his wife or an assistant will take you out the back or out the front and unlock the store room which serves as the shop. In here there is much rummaging in the deep gloom to discover what is available. The choice is invariably strictly limited. Prices are always high, due to haulage charges. Quality of perishable items is best not discussed at all.

In the bar itself, beer does not come in glasses via taps. It is sold by the bottle or can and things being what they are, is not always refrigerated. A request for a beer off the ice may be met with the reply: "Here y'are, mate, a thousand miles off the ice!"

Our bush railway system,
what there is of it, caters
for goods rather than passengers.
Few railway lines service
the far Outback.
The most recent major
improvement was the linking
of Alice Springs with
Adelaide in 1929

**Selected Aboriginal stockmen
on the government-run
Haasts Bluff Reserve, which
is operated as a cattle station,
live in aluminium huts
like this one**

No matter how unlikely its appearance, provided it is not actually abandoned, the far outback pub nearly always serves meals. I can recommend the cuisine at Betoota, Birdsville, Tibooburra, and Marree.

You rarely find a garage in these last pub-and-store towns, but petrol can often be obtained by a call at the local oil company agent's home. He usually has a few drums lying around the back yard.

If you can locate him or his wife, which can take some time, they will open a drum, drop in a hand pump, and invite you to pump out what you like. Until recently, petrol in places like Betoota cost anything up to 80 cents a gallon, but price rationalization schemes have brought it down very close to city prices.

When there is a garage in a far outback town, it is often shut, because the owner is away for a few days somewhere. No one can be sure when he will be back. When there is no garage, there is usually someone reputed to be a handy mechanic living near by. He may be out of town, too.

The police station is usually the best source of local information on almost any subject. No matter how small the town, there is almost invariably a police station. Unfortunately, the policeman is often away somewhere, too.

The lack of services for travellers at

these small settlements is readily explained. The towns do not exist for the benefit of travellers, but for the convenience of local residents. Income derived from passers-by would rarely amount to a significant percentage of turnover.

Such towns are no more than handy depots for delivery of goods destined for stations in the area. Only the pub and police station dispense anything—in the first instance, grog, and in the second, justice. The pub in such a town is a meeting place for locals, who see each other perhaps only a couple of times a year. This means they are kept busy exchanging news when they meet and the publican is kept busy listening. A stranger may be ignored and go away with the impression that outback dwellers are aloof and stand-offish.

But if a traveller happens into town when the bar is almost empty, he will probably find the barman or his sole fellow drinker as talkative as he is.

There is little social or community life

any more in these towns. You need people in numbers for that. The best that can be managed is an occasional bar room song or brawl, when a bunch of drovers or station hands come into town.

In the larger outback towns, those boasting a pub *and* a store (such as Wanaaring or Marree), there is usually a cluster of town houses within sight of the business community. There may be anything from half a dozen to a score of buildings. Some of them will be little more than humpies, a few will be recognizably tradesmen built, if not pretentious, and one or two will be comfortable looking small homesteads, with wide verandas, trellised, and fly-wired, and low roof lines.

All but the last mentioned dwellings will be badly in need of paint and general repairs, having a markedly down-at-heel appearance by city standards. Few if any will have any semblance of a garden. The

**An Aboriginal teacher
at a government school in
the Northern Territory**

neatest homes in this group will belong to
the policeman, the Pastures Protection
Board inspector, and the school master,
if there is one.

The one or two bigger homes, with
gardens and perhaps even a few square
feet of lawn, will belong to a retired
squatter come to live out his days in town
(his sons run the property now), or a not-
much-seen retired haulage contractor or
builder, or his widow.

Lessons in the sunshine
outside the modern school at
Papunyah Aboriginal Reserve,
west of Alice Springs

**Pupils work
on a project in
their classroom
at the Yuendemu
Aboriginal
Reserve school**

HOTEL
POST OFFICE BROKEN HILL

A walk in the
perennial sunshine
of Broken Hill,
capital city of
New South Wales'
far Outback

Dreaming in the sun
at Marree, outside the
town's single store

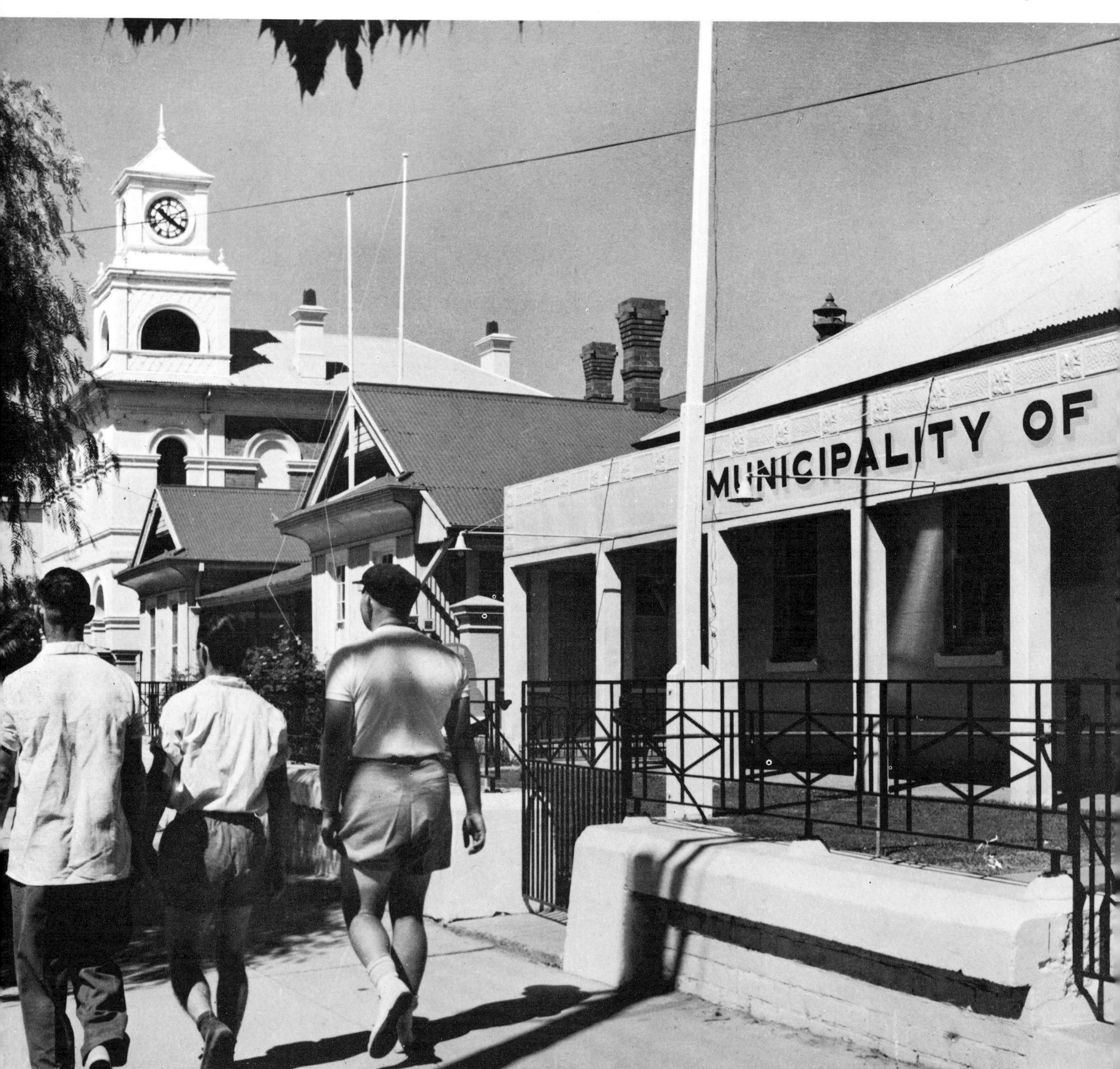

Hay, on the
lower Murrumbidgee River,
is an historic town
on the border of
the true Outback.
Banjo Paterson made it
famous in his poem
"Hay, Hell, and Booligal"

A very few outback towns boast new buildings, often of aluminium prefabrication, scientifically designed for climate and conditions, which have been built to eradicate a social problem. The oldtimers' cottages at Birdsville (built by the Australian Inland Mission for pensioners) fall into this class. So does the students' hostel at Tibooburra. But these are the exceptions, rather than the rule.

Most of the time the single main streets of these towns are as empty as the Nullarbor Plain, but at certain times on certain days, as many as a dozen citizens may be seen at the one time. These are mail and pension days.

Nine-tenths of the crowd will be made up of Aborigines, Afghans, and half-castes. There will be a big percentage of children. If it is pension day, there will be people on the street for hours, wandering in and out of store, hotel, and perhaps the garage, if there is one. All-white citizens wait until the hubbub is over, then pop in and out of the post office quickly and back to the security of their homes. Their shopping can wait until later, when there is less of the raggle taggle of humanity in the store.

The big perimeter or mining towns of the Outback, like Broken Hill, Bourke, Charleville, and so on, don't differ much from the large rural towns in the more

To many people, the town of Bourke, in north-west New South Wales symbolizes the Outback. But most of the territory discussed in this book lies ''back o' Bourke''

A fine example of
outback station architecture . . .
Muloorina homestead,
at the southern tip
of Lake Eyre in
South Australia

Inside the big kitchen
at Curtin Springs Station
near Ayers Rock
in the Northern Territory.
Once primarily a grazing
property, this station
caters increasingly for
tourists, providing meals
and accommodation

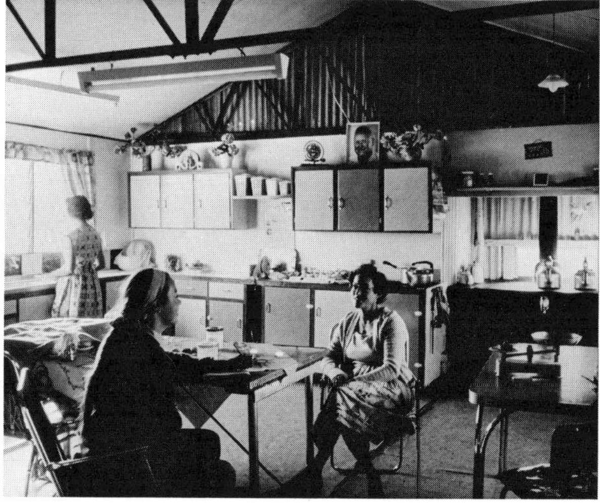

favoured areas. Not quite so splendid or well found as, say, Wagga, they are moderately prosperous centres with few surprises, delights, or disappointments.

They all have at least one paved street, and numerous pubs, shops, banks, garages, and cafés. Their most interesting feature, to the visitor, is their sharply defined colour bar. A quick tour of shops, cafés, pubs, the town baths, and picture shows illustrates the sharp boundaries of racial discrimination.

The social and community life of these larger towns is well organized and varied. They all have their bowling, cricket, football, and tennis clubs, their R.S.L., church groups, Rotarians, Lions, Country Women's Association, progress association, parents' and citizens' association, and Chamber of Commerce. Few black, brown, or coffee-coloured citizens belong to these organizations, much less hold offices. Their only society is that for the underprivileged, with headquarters at a safe distance out of town, in humpy-ville.

But for the casual visitor, who observes only the obvious, the large outback towns are pleasant places in which to shake out and wash down the dust of the track.

Although it is not the biggest, Alice Springs is by far the best known and most refreshingly different town in the Outback. Its reputation as a place worth seeing is fully justified. There really is no place like Alice.

The difference, and attraction, lies in the fact that Alice Springs is primarily a tourist town.

This is Alice Springs
from the air, looking south
toward The Gap.
Busy, progressive, and
expanding, the town nevertheless
remains an insignificant
speck on a landscape so
vast as to be almost
beyond comprehension

Strollers and shoppers in an arcade of modern shops of the town's main street

Dust haze like this has become an increasingly common sight in Alice Springs since the turn of the century. While grazing continues, the hazard will worsen. This is Todd Street, the town's shopping centre

'ASPRO'
for yours
NOW!
'ASPRO'
6
for colds and flu
headache and pain
Bex
Bex
Powders
Bex
Bex
Powders
ESPRESSO   COFFEE   1/6   ITALIAN   CORDIALS   1/

It caters for visitors—and depends on them largely for its existence. The other "big" towns of the Outback, like the tiny one-pub-cum-store settlements, exist largely for the benefit of the local community. There is nothing wrong with this—the same could be said of Melbourne or Sydney.

But for the tourist, although Cunnamulla or Camooweal may be the more fair dinkum article, the best choice is Alice Springs. There he will see what he expects to see in an outback town: stockmen of every size, shape, and colour, road trains, opals, flying doctors . . . the lot. And all in air-conditioned comfort amid a variety of scenic attractions that have no equal anywhere in Australia.

To me, tourism of the Alice Springs kind represents the most desirable form of development for the Australian Outback. It is the one place in the Outback where men are putting something into the country and reaping a safe harvest.

Left:
**New Australians have
penetrated to every corner
of the Outback,
usually in the role
of shopkeepers**

Below:
**The classic façade of
the true large outback town . . .
pub, stock and station agent,
and bank, in that order**

THE ECONOMY

Previous page:
**Artesian water has made
intensive grazing possible in dry,
sparsely vegetated country
never intended for grazing by
nature. Artesian pressure is
already down by 70 per cent and
daily output is dwindling.
Nature's unwelcome guests will
eventually have to go**

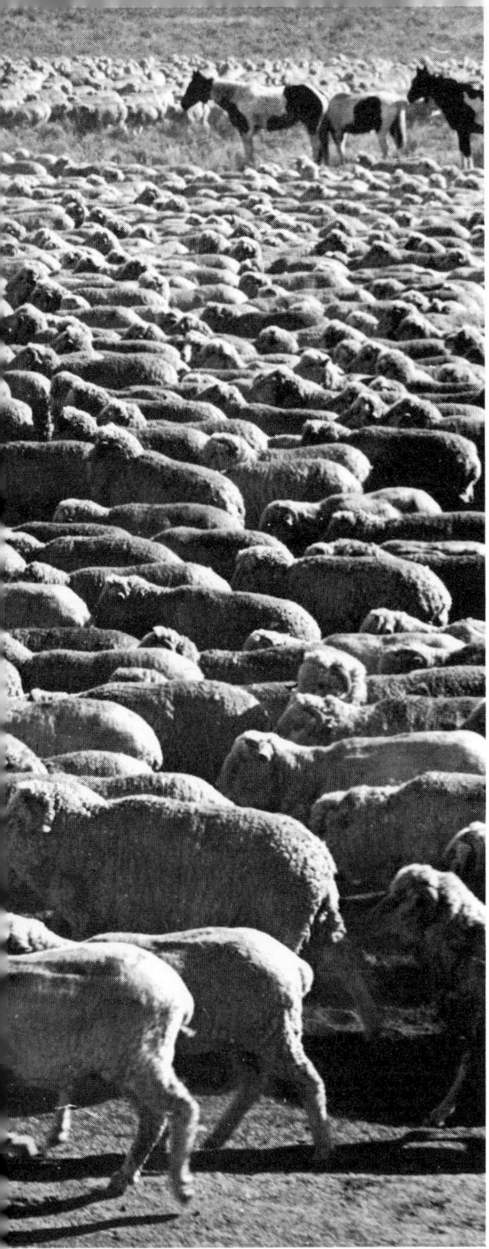

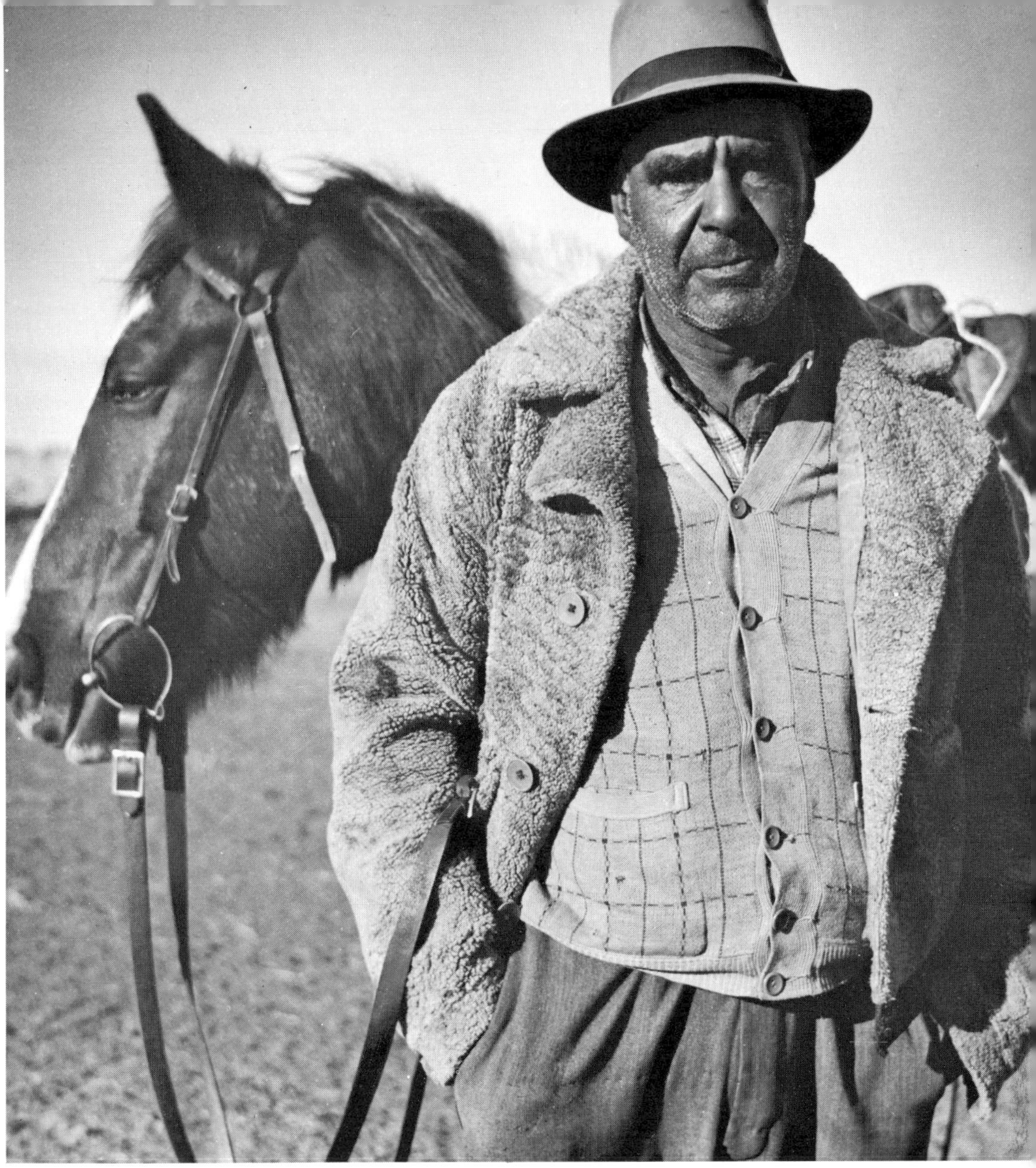

Left:
A mob of 6,000 sheep travelling on a stock route in far western New South Wales. Due to lack of feed on the home run, these sheep had been travelling almost a year and had been shorn once along the track

Right:
Aboriginal stockmen and drovers have always been the backbone of the grazing industry, particularly in the cattle country of the north. Their value has rarely been reflected in their pay packets

The economy of the Outback has traditionally been grazing and mining. In most places, towns like Broken Hill, Tennant Creek, Mount Isa, and Kalgoorlie excepted, mining fizzled out.

Grazing has remained, but only barely survives on a permanent basis in most of what I have defined as the real Outback. Graziers have retreated permanently from thousands of square miles of country in the last half century. Ruined homesteads, buried fences, and ghost towns attest to this, and they will be forced to retreat from more and more country as the years go by. This is because the grazing process on which they depend is causing slow but steady deterioration of both cattle and sheep lands.

"When the rains come
things will be okay again."
Sometimes, but not always.
Rain has fallen in this eaten-out
eroded area, but no new
plants or grasses sprout

Shearers race the clock
and each other to improve
their daily tallies,
and are paid so
much per hundred sheep.
Shearers dread "sandy cobblers."
Squatters dread the
call for "tar!"

The presser is a
vital man in any shearing team.
His careless marking of
bales or mixing of classed
lots can reduce the
squatter's wool cheque

Rich, high rainfall country, bolstered with introduced pastures and fertilizers, can be grazed indefinitely, on a rotational basis. Sandy, low rainfall country, struggling at most times to support a sparse covering of native vegetation, cannot be grazed indefinitely.

Experience, not theory, has proved this. The New South Wales Royal Commission on Western Lands (Deterioration) of 1890 and the South Australian Pastoral Acts of 1893-1896 acknowledged this years ago. The first recommended much lower stocking rates and the second prohibited the re-introduction of stock on to ruined grazing land in the north-east of the state.

Plenty of scientific investigations and

Watering the mob at
a tank in sandhill country
on Frome Downs Station,
South Australia

A horse tailer
fills the cook's
pack saddle canteen with
water for the camp
from the same tank

The 6,000 mile long
Wild Dog Fence keeps dingoes out
of the remote sheeplands
of South Australia, New South Wales,
and Queensland. Gates every
30 miles are supposed to
be kept shut, or else!

Cutting out a beast during
a muster near the boundaries of
Frome Downs and Quinyambie Stations
in South Australia. Stock on
these largely unfenced runs
intermingle and have to be sorted
out before "fats" can be
sent away with drovers

surveys in recent times confirm that many native grasses, shrubs, and trees are being eaten down to the point of no recovery—and that they are being replaced with weeds unpalatable to stock. Anyone who runs a few backyard fowls knows the process: after a while nothing grows in the fowlyard except weeds.

Many outback graziers disagree with the claim that their lands are deteriorating. When their cattle die and they are forced temporarily or permanently off their land, they blame drought and say the land will come good again after rain.

Botanists, agronomists, and other soil scientists have written numerous papers,

Kangaroos once thrived
inside the protection of the dingo
fence, but in the last decade,
professional shooters have
drastically reduced their numbers.
Conservationists fear
for their survival

based on lengthy and extensive surveys, indicating that the graziers are wrong and that outback land and vegetation are deteriorating. I have a shelf full of scientific reports to quote from.

No grazier has yet backed his claims by quoting a scientific source. Some have quoted statistics showing there are now more sheep and cattle per square mile on some properties than there used to be. They see this as proof that land cannot be deteriorating. But the argument doesn't stand up to investigation.

New bores put down during the last twenty years or so have enabled stock to graze country that was previously beyond

Pegging out 'roo skins in far
western New South Wales.
In recent years the demand
has been for carcases, as
well as skins, for
use as pets' meat

its range from existing watering points. Many properties today are grazing land that is comparatively newly opened up. On the same properties there will be square miles of barren, eaten-out country around the old bores put down in earlier days.

It is only a matter of time before most of the country now being grazed in the Outback reaches the sorry state of the already abandoned cattle and sheep runs.

The economy of the Outback will no doubt remain heavily dependent on the pastoral industry for the next twenty years or so. No one, not even their harshest critic, expects graziers to pull up their stakes and leave tomorrow. But it is important that today's cattle and sheep men should begin planning for the day when their sons move into a different form of land utilization—or get out.

It is purely a matter of self preservation,

Broad axes have been
traditional tools of trade
in the bush since
the pioneer days. They
are still used by some sleeper
and bridge timber cutters

Mobile power saws
like this one
have replaced axes
and wedges in most places.
This man is cutting
red gum sleepers

for the individuals concerned and for the nation in general. Deserts, once on the march, are hard to stop.

At present, the outback pastoral industry is of little significance on a national scale.

The Alice Springs pastoral district produces an average of only 50,000 animals each year. The famous Channel Country of south-western Queensland fattens about the same number. Far outback New South Wales and adjacent cattle country in South Australia between them produce less than 20,000 marketable animals yearly.

Add on a generous estimate of 30,000 for cattle marketed by remote country stations in Western Australia (excluding the rich Kimberley area), and the total is a mere 150,000 animals. Out of the total number of 7 million cattle slaughtered in Australia each year, this represents something like $1\frac{1}{2}$ per cent. Hardly significant on a national scale.

The far outback sheep industry is similarly tiny when viewed against the nation's total wool industry. There are only 1,000,000 sheep in the Western Division of New South Wales, which covers almost half the state. Queensland's far outback stations graze no more than 1,500,000. South Australia, Western Australia, and the Northern Territory between them would run no more than 500,000 sheep on dry marginal country.

This gives a total of 2,000,000 sheep. Australia's total sheep population is over 160,000,000. So the outback sheep, which are causing serious and continuing land deterioration, represent only $1\frac{1}{4}$ per cent of the nation's sheep population.

The far outback pastoral industry amounts to this: $1\frac{1}{2}$ per cent of our cattle and $1\frac{1}{4}$ per cent of our sheep are slowly but inexorably bringing about the ruination of almost half the Australian continent. From the nation's point of view, it is simply not worth it.

Mining has always been the second most important factor in the economy of the Outback. The traditional centres have been Broken Hill, Mount Isa, Tennant Creek, and Kalgoorlie, producing chiefly lead, silver, zinc, copper, and gold. In recent years, more and more mineral discoveries have been made. The present rate of prospecting indicates that further strikes of products—solid, liquid, and gaseous—will be made.

There is now a large open-cut coal mine at Leigh Creek, in north-eastern South Australia, not far from Marree. Gas has been discovered at Gidgealpa and Moomba in South Australia, at Gilmore in central western Queensland and at Mereenie, south-west of Alice Springs in the Northern Territory. There have been new finds of nickel in the Tomkinson and Blackstone Ranges, straddling the Western Australian border, south-west of Ayers Rock. There is manganese at Mount Sydney in Western Australia, and huge iron ore deposits at Mount Newman and Mount Tom Price are now being developed.

It seems only a matter of time before oil is discovered in the far Outback. Strikes have already been made at closer-in places like Moonee.

Mining seems destined to become the cornerstone of Australia's outback economy. It already outstrips grazing, the traditional money-earner, in many areas. For example, mine products in the Northern Territory are now valued at above $8,000,000 annually, compared with $7,000,000 for beef cattle.

Unlike grazing, the mining industry does little damage to the country, except to leave a few large, unsightly holes in the ground. It is infinitely preferable to grazing.

Tourism has become increasingly important to the economy of the Outback in recent years. This is particularly so in the Alice Springs area, where it has already outstripped grazing as a money earner. This is doubly impressive when you consider that while the local pastoral industry is more than half a century old, tourism is just out of its first decade.

The Alice Springs district has the Outback's greatest concentration of spectacular scenic attractions, but tourism is developing in other places. There are now guided tours along the Birdsville Track. Four-wheel-drive safaris visit such historic places as the "DIG" tree on Cooper Creek.

The Corner Country of north-west New South Wales, one of the few places where red kangaroos and emus are still seen in numbers, has been discovered by several tour operators. Languishing Tibooburra may yet be revived as a replica of a goldrush town in the rip-snorting days of last century. The near-by ruins of Milparinka may again ring to the sound of prospectors' picks, swung by picture-taking tourists.

Water pipelines like this one between Menindie Lakes and Broken Hill are the lifelines of some outback mining towns. To date, piping water long distances for agriculture has proved uneconomical. The idea holds little future prospect

Irrigation schemes require
a vast supply of cheap water.
In the far Outback,
annual evaporation rates
in the order of 8 feet
would cause phenomenal waste.
Even cheap water would be
prohibitively expensive

Right:
Mining has brought
prosperity and permanence
to many outback centres.
The future of outback
mining seems bright

The ailing cattle stations of the Cooper and Diamantina country may get a new lease of life as dude ranches, after the pattern of Ross River, near Alice Springs. And sooner or later someone will realize the colossal tourist potential of Lake Eyre and the Simpson Desert. Helicopter safaris will camp one night amid red sandhills and the next on a limitless plain of rock-hard salt. For the more intrepid tourists there will be rubber-wheeled sail "boats" for an exhilarating trip down Bluebird's world record-breaking track.

The winds of change are blowing in the Outback. The squatter's hat on the peg is flanked by the hard-hats of miners and the fly-veiled caps of the tourists. From any angle, the change is for the better.

Opals are a rare form of
wealth garnered from the earth of
the Outback. Coober Pedy and
Andamooka are the chief producers.
Some gougers still work at
Lightning Ridge and White Cliffs, in
New South Wales. These specimens
are from the famous collection
of Mrs Jenkins, proprietor
of ''The Ritz'' in Alice Springs

Much has been written about the Aranda school of water colour painting in central Australia. Many have debated its validity. Its defenders say that long before the arrival of European-trained painters, the traditional Aranda art had become so stylized, with its rigid geometric symbolism and inter-relation with story-telling, that it had "gone as far as it could go." Therefore, it seems natural that a vigorous school of water-colourists rose to follow the example of the late Albert Namatjira. Some of the Aranda artists may be mere copyists, but others, experts agree, produce vital and original work which strongly reflects their traditional background.

Tourists discuss their proposed purchase of an Aboriginal water colour with the director of Alice Springs' Tmara Mara art gallery

Below:
Rex Battarbee, owner of the gallery, encouraged Albert Namatjira to take up painting and helped found the Aranda school of water-colourists

Opposite:
Benjamin Landara, one of the most successful Aranda artists today, at work under a bush near Alice Springs. He married Albert Namatjira's daughter

Aborigines expressed their art in painting, carving, and engraving, depending on the materials available in the regions where they lived. Their visual art was correlated with their tribal ceremonies. Combination of realistic figures with mystical designs was common. According to E. P. Elkin, Emeritus Professor at Sydney University, this was an "ordered arrangement of symbols, symbolic actions, designs, and sounds . . . to express in outward forms the 'shade', the inner life and meaning, the permanent element in man and the world in the present, past, and future." No longer is Aboriginal art dismissed as merely savage or childlike.

Left:
Tourists on a guided tour of the caves around the base of Ayers Rock. Some were once sacred places to the Aborigines, who have kept away since the coming of the white man

Below:
Detail shows an Aboriginal artist's impression of a man on horseback, plus a hatted, standing figure, probably a European

Below:
A party of youthful tourists in Standley Chasm at noon. Walls glow brilliantly for only a few minutes each day, when sun strikes into the gorge at midday

Tourists atop Ayers Rock.
Often the brilliance
of their clothing
outshines the famed colours
of the Centre

A young camel watches
disinterestedly as a tour
bus departs from
Mount Ebeneer Chalet,
bound for Ayers Rock

Fly-veiled tourists
watch doubtfully as a
guide cuts fresh damper
for their morning tea at
Ross River dude ranch

On post cards, Ayers Rock
looks colourful, but unimpressive.
In reality it is enormous, its
colour less brilliant. These
tourists are scarcely half way up
"The Climb" to the summit

THE WILDLIFE

The native animals, birds, and reptiles of the Outback are valuable and irreplaceable natural resources. They are among our major tourist attractions. The underground natural resources of the Outback may be worth more in hard cash—but when all the coal and iron has been dug up, more will surely be found in other parts of the world.

When the last emu or kangaroo dies, the species is finished. We will not discover more in South America or Africa or China. These unique creatures will be gone from the face of the earth for ever.

Outback Australia was never rich in wildlife, in the accepted sense. No great herds grazed the saltbush and Mitchell grass plains of our Inland. The mulga and corkwood trees never sheltered colonies of chattering, furred creatures.

Perhaps in some dim, dark age things were different. But since the inland seas dried up and the landscape became parched, only a comparative handful of

Left above:
A male red kangaroo on the move in north-western New South Wales. Professional shooters could wipe out this species

Left lower:
Brolgas in flight over the Channel Country of far west Queensland. They are not common in the Outback, but may be seen from the Murray River to Arnhem Land

Right:
Buffalo on the move. Estimates put the population of these introduced animals at around half a million

Previous page:
Major Mitchell parrots in flight near Lake Eyre, in the desert country of South Australia

rare creatures have survived in our semi-arid hinterland.

Fortunately for them, Australia was set adrift from the rest of the world before the large predator animals of Africa, Asia, and Europe roamed this far. Our emus, kangaroos, and lesser marsupials would have been no match for Africa's lions or India's tigers.

Outback Australia today is a sort of living museum, populated by animals long since extinct in other parts of the world. The whole continent was in this category before white men came here—but almost two centuries of wholesale destruction of wildlife and its natural habitat has changed the scene drastically.

To quote just one example: in the settled areas of Australia, nearly 50 per cent of all marsupial species are now extinct; the surviving species are mostly classified as rare and live a twilight existence in remote, inaccessible areas or in wildlife refuges.

**Buffalo on the swampy plains
of the Northern Territory**

Top right:
Mountain devil photographed
near the southern
perimeter of Tanami Desert, in
the Northern Territory

Saltwater crocodiles
in northern Australia were
once slaughtered indiscriminately.
Now they are being
conserved and a permit is
necessary to shoot one.
Freshwater crocodiles are
completely protected

A young visitor to Muloorina
Station in South Australia puzzles
over a line of processionary
caterpillars. Leaf eaters,
they are on their way from
one tree to another

Today's citizens of places like Sydney or Melbourne are surprised to learn that emus, kangaroos, and pied geese used to live where their cities now stand.

For many years these creatures have been easy to see only in the remoter parts of the eastern states. This has given rise to the popular notion that they were always outback dwellers. The fallacy of this convenient attitude is worth pointing out, because Australians need to be aware that our wildlife is on the retreat to the last great sanctuary available—the remote Outback.

But even this sanctuary is now threatened.

As more and better roads, railways, and aircraft landing grounds are developed, the Outback becomes less of a sanctuary for wildlife. Professional hunters, using four-wheel-drive vehicles, are ranging further afield into country that was previously inaccessible to them.

Oil drilling and mining companies are building roads which later develop into tourist highways. Among the tourists are always plenty of sportsmen with guns.

New equipment and methods have made it possible to put down bores in harsh country, so that cattle and sheep can be introduced. These animals eventually eat down the native herbage on which the wildlife depends for food and shelter. When dry times come, drovers or road trains take the sheep or cattle away, but the native animals remain to perish. Survivors are exterminated as pests.

During more than a decade of travel in the Outback, I have seen wildlife numbers

A grazier west of
Bourke spars with a
giant red kangaroo he
has just chased to
the point of exhaustion
in a Jeep

A male kangaroo
and a youngster stare at
the camera from
a stony ridge near
Tibooburra in
the Corner Country of
New South Wales

dwindle steadily in those areas where new roads have been established or old tracks improved. Ten years ago, for example, the Wanaaring to Tibooburra track in north-west New South Wales was a route used rarely except by locals. In those days, kangaroos were visible in numbers every few miles. At dusk or early morning when they were feeding, you could drive to within 50 yards of a mob, get out quietly, and take pictures.

If I camped overnight, there was a regular thudding of marsupial feet as kangaroos bounded past, not far beyond the limits of the firelight. In the morning I was often awakened by the clicking sound of emus picking at the shiny glass of my Land-Rover's headlights.

Today the Wanaaring-Tibooburra track is regularly graded and you count yourself lucky to see one or two emus or kangaroos during the whole 140-mile trip.

Three pelicans confer in midstream on Cooper Creek

Not far away, a group of tortoises sun themselves on a safely isolated log

Downstream, three spoonbills enjoy similar pleasures, also safely midstream

With no friends and
plenty of enemies, the dingo
is the lone wolf of the
Outback. He can cause
ruinous losses to sheepmen and
has cost the nation
millions of dollars in
eradication programmes
over the years

The waterholes of the Cooper, the Diamantina, and other outback streams are not as inaccessible as they used to be. There are organized tours to Birdsville these days—and four-wheel-drive safaris to Cooper Creek and other remote creeks or swamps where wildlife, particularly wildfowl, still thrive.

In such places it is possible to see the air thick with birds, large and small, and to watch kangaroos, emus, and other wild creatures drinking almost side by side. Pelicans herd fish in the shallows; long-legged spoonbills dabble in the marshes; finches, cockatoos, and galahs teem in the coolibahs; emus, a score at a time, run helter-skelter through the mulga and salt-bush; kangaroos stand up and look inquisitively, instead of instantly fleeing. The wily dingo trots around the camp, at a respectable distance, like a tame dog.

There are few enough such cases in the Outback. It is only a matter of time before most of them are made easily accessible to the travelling public. Unless steps are taken now to protect them, it is just as inevitable that within the next decade their wildlife populations will dwindle—as those along the improved Wanaaring track have dwindled.

I would like to see all large outback waterholes, billabongs, and swamps declared complete wildlife refuges. Those near roads or tracks could be partly fenced so that travellers would have access to no more than about a fifth of the whole area. This would give the birds and animals a haven of retreat and ensure that their nests or lairs were never disturbed.

Livestock such as sheep and cattle would need to be fenced out of each refuge, preferably by a margin of several miles. The fences would need wildlife gates at intervals to provide free access for native animals but not introduced livestock. Tourist-proof fences would be needed where the road passed through or beside the waterhole sanctuary. A quarter mile of fencing in each direction from popular stopping places would be enough. Tourists seldom walk more than a few hundred yards.

The carrying of guns, nets, or traps within a prescribed number of miles of a waterhole refuge could be prohibited. Ideally, I would like to see the entire outback area discussed in this book declared a complete wildlife refuge. The possession of traps, snares, or nets would be illegal. The carrying of firearms by non-resident travellers would be prohibited. Residents of the Outback are entitled to own and carry firearms, because they are a necessary part of station life—for the despatching of injured or diseased livestock, the killing of cattle for beef, and the destruction of the occasional marauding dingo or fox.

I know that some outback residents are major offenders in the destruction of wildlife for sport or under the guise of pest eradication. But resident wildlife wardens in the Outback could deal more effectively with these hooligans than an unjust and universally reviled firearm prohibition.

If tourists knew that patrolling wildlife wardens had the right to examine their vehicles for firearms, they would soon give

The jabiro or
policeman bird of the
Outback keeps watch
over grazing wildlife
from a commanding
vantage point.
If there is a
disturbance among a flock
of feeding birds,
he will swoop down and
admonish them.
If danger approaches,
he sets up a
warning commotion

up carrying them. A resident wildlife warden would know all vehicles in his district, even if it covered several thousand square miles—because there are so few of them. So he wouldn't waste time or build up local illwill by examining vehicles belonging to local drivers.

On the other hand, bush communities being what they are, he would soon get to hear of any poaching exploits by district residents. Wildlife wardens posted at Wilcannia, Wanaaring, Tibooburra, Quilpie, Birdsville, and Marree could effectively protect wildlife (from guns and traps) in an area of some 250,000 square miles. Another man at Boulia, Duchess, Tennant Creek, and Alice Springs would complete the "mantle of safety" for wildlife that is needed in the Outback now.

Later, when more travellers are on the roads of outback Western Australia, wildlife wardens will be needed in some of the isolated settlements of that state.

The other major form of protection needed by outback wildlife concerns their natural habitat. This is being steadily debased by introduced grazing animals such as sheep, cattle, aided and abetted by wild horses, goats, and rabbits. I have already stated elsewhere in this book what I think should be done about the first two species mentioned. If and when they are withdrawn from our semi-arid Outback, the remaining brumbies and goats could be mopped up by government hunters in the same way as New Zealand has undertaken red deer eradication. By that time, the introduction of the rabbit flea as a

The Johnston or
freshwater crocodile is small
compared with *Porosis,* the saltwater
species, and harmless to man.
It is protected

Strange walking fish
of the north are found on
the mudbanks of tidal
rivers in Queensland and
the Northern Territory

Photographed at dusk
on Mount Wood Station, near
Tibooburra in north-west New South Wales
this mother kangaroo and joey
appear to be grazing almost
bare earth.
Closer examination of
the ground (right), shows a
fresh green pick of onion grass and
other native succulents.
Tiny and dust-coated,
these little green shoots are
scarcely noticed by the
untrained human eye

carrier of myxomatosis will probably have dealt with the final problem.

Meanwhile, all visitors to the Outback could bear in mind that many of the wild creatures they encounter beside the track are more than just interestingly different birds and animals. In many cases they are the last surviving specimens of some of the world's most unique wildlife.

To participate in their destruction, or countenance their destruction by others, is on a par with running riot with an axe in an art gallery or museum. Such creatures as the kangaroo or the emu, "millions of years in the making," are the living counterparts of the inanimate art treasures of Cellini and Leonardo.

Emus pace the author's Land-Rover along a dog-proof fence north of Cockburn in South Australia

The proverbial shag on the rock

135

14-741

TRAVEL

Previous page:
**Land-Rover in dust storm
near Alice Springs**

Left:
**Kangaroo prints across
a salt lake will
remain until next rain,
perhaps years away**

Centre:
**Land-Rover cuts
deep tracks to the
crest of a red outback
sand ridge**

Right:
**Navigating in the
featureless gibber
plains of Sturt's
Stony Desert**

DANGER High Voltage

The size of the Australian Outback and the everyday problems of travelling from place to place are beyond the understanding of anyone who hasn't been there. The distances involved are colossal, but more important is the primitive condition of what roads there are.

Most of them are just bush tracks that often disappear in sand dunes, creek beds, or on stony rises. Apart from the bitumen-surfaced Barkly and Stuart highways (which are only wide enough for one car in many parts), there is scarcely a road worthy of the name in the entire Outback. They are just as scarce as permanent rivers. The best of them are reasonable for a few weeks after grading but they quickly deteriorate into their usual corrugated, lumpy condition.

Aircraft now carry many tourists, most businessmen, and the flying doctor, but the basic form of transport for outback dwellers today is still the motor vehicle. Most personal transport and practically all heavy transport is via roads and tracks. Very often these routes are the old camel and bullock tracks of yesteryear, only slightly widened and improved since grand-dad's day.

In many places, transport is no more certain and not much quicker than it was almost a century ago. In fact, a flooded creek or a boggy plain will stop a truck more effectively than it would a string of camels.

Bridges or elevated roads remain virtually unknown in the far Outback. So do regularly graded gravel surfaces.

Top Left:
The sand dunes of the Outback are colourful camera subjects, but car stoppers, too

Left:
A prankster's grim quip on outback motoring, beside the lonely track to Lake Eyre

This is a "good" outback road, regularly graded to provide access to an oil drilling rig in south-west Queensland. When the drillers move on, it will quickly deteriorate

Bullock teams helped open
up the Outback, hauling in food
and building supplies,
hauling out wool bales.
Now working bullocks
are almost unknown

Camels took over from bullocks
in the more arid portions
of the Outback, but
now they are used chiefly by
wandering Aboriginal tribes
or as tourist gimmicks

In the old days, transport was slow but fairly sure. Everything went by camel train or bullock dray. Horse-drawn wagons were used on the better tracks. Personal transport was by camel or saddle horse, with gear stowed on a pack animal strung behind.

The early explorers used horses, bullocks, and later camels to cross the continent from north to south and east to west. In 1846, Leichhardt took a bullock all the way from Queensland to Port Essington, on the north-west tip of what is now Arnhem Land. Burke and Wills used horses and camels on their tragic journey of 1861. Ernest Giles, aided by nineteen camels, crossed the Great Victoria Desert to Western Australia in 1875.

In those days and right up until the 1920s, far-out stations received most of their supplies annually. Items like tea came in hundred-weight chests, flour and sugar by the ton. If supplies were more than a few weeks late, settlers rode off down the track to find out what was up. It was either that or starve.

Sometimes they rode hundreds of miles to the railhead towns of Oodnadatta or Marree, to find perhaps that the Afghan camel driver had died on the track—or that a train had been derailed hundreds of miles south and supplies were being brought up on bullock teams. Then it was a case of

Road train
on the Stuart Highway,
Northern Territory

A typical outback road.
Such tracks often fork many
times, without signposts,
to the consternation of visiting
motorists. (This "road" is
clearly marked on the
map of Australia!)

The road to Adelaide,
just south of Alice Spring
It is roughly 1,000 miles
to the bitumen surface
at Port Augusta

wait, or go down the line and lend a hand.

Some of the old camel and bullock teams hauled prodigious loads. Horses did their share of the work, too. Up to fifty were used in a team. In the 1890s, a thirty-eight-horse team hauled a 16-ton boiler from Oodnadatta railhead to the gold mining town of Arltunga, north-east of Alice Springs. This was a journey of some 400 miles through sandhills and across claypans and gibber plains.

Camels hauled corrugated iron and other building materials from Marree to Birdsville, a journey of 325 miles through some of the toughest country in the Aust-ralian Outback. From the sheep country of western New South Wales, wool bales went via camel, bullock, and horse teams down to the riverboats of the Murray.

Transport by camel or bullock team was excruciatingly slow, but moderately sure. Rain sometimes upset timetables, but in

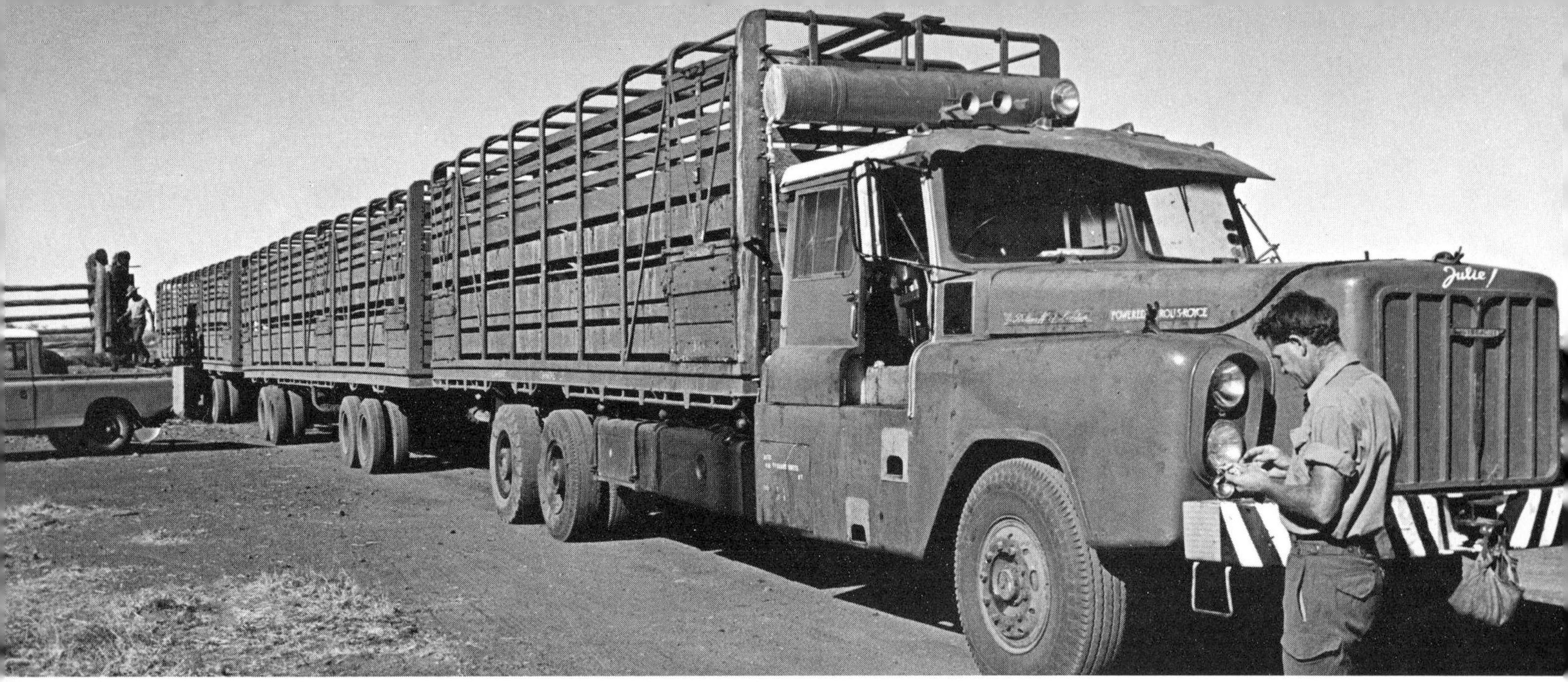

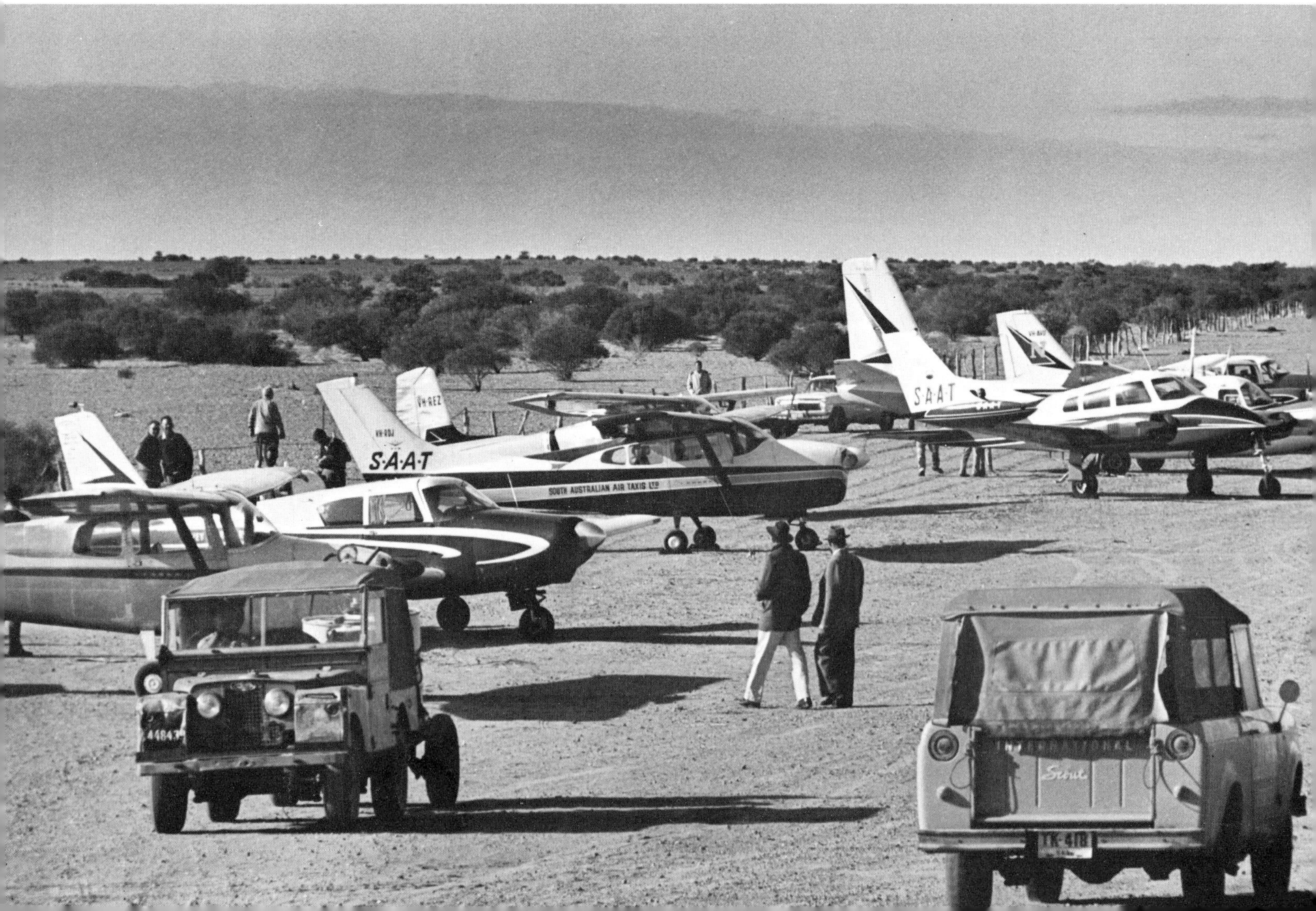
S·A·A·T
SOUTH AUSTRALIAN AIR TAXIS LTD
S·A·A·T

A road train driver checks
his vehicle before setting out
from Helen Springs, on the
Stuart Highway, for the
railhead at Mount Isa, some
500 miles away. His load
of cattle then face a
further 600-mile rail
journey to the coast

Air travel is popular
in the Outback, but conventional
planes require airstrips that
are expensive to establish
and maintain. Helicopters, large
and small, could solve
most of the Outback's
transport problems

Since 1929, radio
has made life easier for
outback dwellers. In recent
years, portable transceivers
have brought inland
travellers under
Flynn's "mantle of safety"

general, outback settlers would know to the day the arrival time of their favourite Afghan hawker on his annual or biannual visit.

A ride in a horse cart from Alice Springs to the railway station at Oodnadatta took two weeks in good times, three weeks after showers, and a month after heavy rain. Really heavy showers were mostly a few years apart, so it was usually safe to reckon on doing the trip in a fortnight.

Cobb and Co., and later the cattle king Sidney Kidman, established coach routes in the outback country of the eastern states. In the hey-day of the six-in-hand teams, it was possible to travel between such places as Charleville, Hungerford, and Broken Hill at the astonishing speed of 150 miles a day.

Motor vehicles eventually undermined this form of transport, after a long hard battle for supremacy. Probably the greatest motoring pioneer was Francis Birtles, who used to send petrol supplies ahead over his proposed routes on camel trains. He was the first man to drive up the notorious Birdsville Track.

Motor vehicles didn't oust horse-drawn coaches from the outback mail and passenger runs because of their speed. For many years they were slower than coaches—and less likely to get through if there was mud or fresh drift sand on the track. But they won out because motor transport required a less complicated and therefore cheaper organization than the coaching business.

All that was needed along the track were drums of fuel, instead of relays of fresh horses and men to handle and feed them, seven days a week.

Over the years, the vehicles used for outback transport have improved tremendously. Today they have more power, more carrying capacity, higher ground clear-

A dusty take-off from
Alice Springs. Locals admit
dust storms are getting
worse and more frequent,
but blame drought rather
than over-grazing

ances, greater comfort and reliability, and up to ten driving wheels. But the tracks on which they operate are for the most part not much better than they were in the days of Kidman's outback coach service.

This is understandable when the size of the Australian Outback is considered. It would cost more than the whole continent is worth to replace every outback track with a good all-weather road.

The growing volume of air transport is an indication of future trends in outback travel. Larger conventional planes and busier timetables will cater for the large outback settlements. But for the small towns and private stations, helicopters may ultimately supply the major form of transport—for passengers, goods, and perhaps, one day, even livestock.

This possible trend may take place as a result of the same circumstances that favoured motor-cars rather than horses and then better vehicles rather than better roads: operating costs.

Just as it is plainly uneconomical to build good roads to every outback homestead, it is equally uneconomical to build on every property an airstrip capable of handling the bigger and faster conventional aircraft that will be flying in the Outback in the near future. Towns and oil or mining companies may be able to afford such facilities, but not individuals.

Every new aircraft in the outback skies reduces the need for the roads and railroads that haven't been built anyway. Every outback station that now runs a tiny Cessna for personal travel but maintains several large trucks for heavy transport points up the need for large transport helicopters to be introduced into the Australian Outback. They are the logical alternative to building and maintaining ruinously costly roads, railways, and conventional airstrips.

Gleaming salt pans,
reflecting the blue sky, giving an
illusion of brimming lakes

Which track? A question often facing the
motorist who is a stranger to
the area. The most-used track is
not always the correct route

Any Australian hunter knows that there are open and closed seasons for most local game, furred and feathered. You can shoot ducks legally only during certain months, and kangaroos only in certain outback locations where they have been officially declared to have reached pest proportions. Emus and many other birds and animals you can't shoot (legally) at all.

But I am no respecter of open or closed seasons. I shoot all the year round, and at anything that gets in my sights, "protected" or otherwise. This is because I shoot only with cameras, not rifles or guns.

This form of hunting is just as exciting and as satisfying as shooting in the conventional sense for sport. And it requires considerably more skill and bushcraft, because the cameraman must come much closer to his quarry than a high-power rifle shooter needs to.

There is even an element of danger in camera-hunting game, particularly in the Northern Territory, when crocodiles or wild buffalo are the quarry. Crocodiles can be approached only by boat. A cameraman laden with gear makes too much noise on land. The only boats available are usually leaky, unstable canoes. In the racing 10-knot current of streams like the East Alligator, these are easily overturned!

Stalking buffalo on foot across open

plains has its exciting moments, too. Most buffalo are docile creatures, but about one in a hundred will charge. As there are over 500,000 buffalo in the Northern Territory, this means there are plenty of potentially dangerous animals to keep a photographer on his toes. Provided you keep down-wind of them, buffalo will often trot straight up to within 50 yards of stationary humans. Then, when they get you in focus, they wheel about and gallop off.

This habit has led to many incorrect stories of buffalo charges, by people who didn't fancy the idea of waiting until the buffalo reached the 50-yard mark. Staring into the "whites" of a buffalo's eyes through a telephoto lens as the animal approaches takes a certain amount of self control. There is always a strong urge to leave the heavy-weight tripod and expensive motor-driven camera and race for the nearest tree. (For buffalo who haven't heard about the 50-yard limit, I rattle a jam tin containing several stones; so far this has always sent them packing.)

Emus are just the opposite. The more unusual the noise and movement the better, where they are concerned. To attract them within range, I have trained my wife, Mare, to lie on the ground and kick her legs in the air, or play them a tune on her recorder.

Kangaroos are extremely shy game and have to be painstakingly stalked. Around sunrise or sundown is the best time, when they are on the move and feeding. In the heat of the day, kangaroos lie down in the shade, often beneath an isolated tree in a large clearing—which makes approaching them difficult. They are doubly wary when dozing and are inclined to snap out of their day-dreaming and bound away at the slightest disturbance.

In timbered country, this means that the first indication you get of the presence of kangaroos is their sudden dash for safety, usually while you are looking the other way.

When they are feeding, however, in the soft light of early morning or late afternoon, they are not so inclined to leave, provided no sudden noise or movement disturbs them. Even when they are aware of your approach, they will often hold their ground, nibbling, while keeping a wary eye on you. You must be down-wind of them, of course, because the smell of humans will send them over the horizon more quickly than anything.

If it becomes necessary to approach kangaroos over open ground, always move directly towards them, preferably against a background of trees or bushes. Never try to circle left or right, once you are visible to them.

This applies to any wild game. Bush creatures, like humans, find it difficult to judge whether or not an object moving directly toward them is really moving at all. The Aborigines and predatory animals like the fox use this principle when stalking their prey.

A vehicle, preferably a four-wheel-drive, is a great help when stalking kangaroos or other camera-shy animals and birds. Provided they haven't recently been shot at from vehicles, wild creatures will usually suffer a car or truck to come much closer than a person on foot. However, unless your vehicle is specially adapted for photography (with drop-down windscreen or an open sun-roof), you will most times have

to get out before taking any photos.

The correct procedure is to halt the vehicle so that the photographer can get out on the side *away* from the quarry and then shoot over the bonnet, using it as a support. Very often the animals or birds will move off very slowly each time the vehicle stops, so that by the time you are ready, they are too far away. It is amazing how often a gully or some other obstacle is between your vehicle and your quarry when this happens. Then the only solution is to continue the stalk on foot.

In suitable country, it is possible to get good action pictures of kangaroos by chasing them in a vehicle. But make no mistake, this is very rough on vehicles. Those outback plains that look so smooth at a distance are usually badly pot-holed and gullied, and strewn with hidden gibbers, cement-hard clay bumps, and indestructible mulga logs. Driving over them is something like driving along between a set of railway tracks, over the sleepers.

The driver needs to be a skilled bush driver, too, or the vehicle, and you, will be damaged severely before the chase is properly under way. It is impossible to drive the vehicle yourself, and take photos.

Realizing this, I used to call in at Romani Station, on the Wanaaring road, west of Bourke, New South Wales, whenever I wanted some good action photos of kangaroos. Don Davey, son of the late Jim Davey, of adjoining Maghera Station used to live there then. Don is now carving out a new empire for himself in Western Australia.

Don is a superb Toyota driver and a kangaroo chaser *par excellence*. We used to chase kangaroos all over Romani and Maghera. Don always enjoyed the driving, but I found picture taking under these conditions about the hardest work I had encountered.

Travelling at 30 to 40 miles an hour over rough claypans, Don's vehicle would leap a foot or so into the air at every bump. There were plenty of bumps. Trying to hold the camera viewfinder against my eye was much the same as bashing my head with a brick. My forehead, nose, and cheek were usually lacerated and bleeding at the end of each run.

I used to stand on the seat of the open vehicle, with one foot braced above the dashboard, just behind the folded-down windscreen. My left arm was looped around a piece of piping above the passenger's door and my right hand held, or rather bumped, my camera against my head.

On really bad bumps, I flew into the air and on the return journey, barked my right shin on the dashboard. When the vehicle crashed into deep gutters, an inexorable downthrust hurled me to the floor, barking my left shin and almost dislocating my left shoulder in the process.

For short bursts, a kangaroo can reach perhaps 35 miles per hour, but he doesn't sustain this for long. When surprised out in the middle of an open plain, a kangaroo naturally enough heads straight for the nearest scrub. A good driver can turn him back into the open. After a few minutes of this, the 'roo slows down to around 20 miles per hour. Then, with luck and good driving, you can manoeuvre close enough to him for good action photos.

After my last visit to Romani Station I gave up chasing kangaroos in vehicles.

Don had been chasing a very large red buck when the animal suddenly swerved directly in front of us and propped in his tracks. Obviously he had decided he couldn't outrun this strange enemy, so he was going to stand and fight!

Don stood heavily on the brakes and I shot forward on to the bonnet, sprawling face down across it. Luckily my boots hooked over the dashboard, anchoring me against further forward progress. As it was, my head and shoulders were slightly overhanging the front bumper bar.

Only a yard away, that magnificent kangaroo struck a fine pose in the whirling dust stirred up by the braking Toyota. I was still clutching at my camera, but what with one thing and another, missed the opportunity to record the dramatic close-up that was offering. Then the 'roo had second thoughts and bounded away.

Mare and I had some more excitement while photographing kangaroos out Tibooburra way. In fact, the experience proved that you can take your life in your hands when you go hunting wildlife with a camera in the Outback. It happened like this.

We were camped on Mount Wood Station, where shooting was prohibited. Kangaroos were plentiful, due to an abundance of green feed brought up by recent storms. Each morning and afternoon we did several hours of 'roo stalking, concentrating on young joeys nibbling the new grass while leaning out of mum's pouch. This sort of photo isn't easy to get under field conditions, but as the days passed, the 'roos seemed to get used to us and we were sometimes able to approach within 50 or 60 yards of them. With our equipment, this was close enough.

Our camp, I should mention, was a very mobile one—in the back of our long wheelbase Land-Rover. At sundown we would simply camp wherever we happened to be. All that was required was to remove some suitcases, camera gear, tucker boxes, and two-way radio from our Dunlopillo mattress in the back, and we were camped.

One night, while we were sleeping in the back of the vehicle, I found myself suddenly awake. Being a light sleeper, this didn't surprise me, and I imagined some faint animal sound or birdcall had disturbed me. But as I was about to put my head down again, I noticed an eerie, sweeping light glowing on and off beneath the distant horizon.

I followed its progress for several minutes, imagining that perhaps I was viewing the mysterious "Min-Min" lights that have puzzled generations of outback settlers.

Sometimes the light would disappear for several minutes, then reappear, far to the left or right. It seemed to be travelling in a weaving motion behind the trees and isolated patches of scrub on the open claypans. It was easy to understand why the Aborigines might have imagined it to be the blazing eye of a giant serpent gliding sinuously over the plain.

At first I judged the light to be the headlights of a car at a great distance, but I knew there were no tracks in that direction —and in any case, the light was moving far too slowly for a vehicle, and following a course more tortuous than any bush track. Once or twice I glimpsed the source of the beam: a single glowing orb, not two, as with a car. But mostly I saw only the sweeping glow of the light, reflecting on

tree trunks and silhouetting clumps of saltbush and mulga.

In the dead silence of the outback night, it was an eerie situation. This was perhaps the lonely, remote atmosphere of the Aborigines' "dream-time," when giant serpents stalked the land.

Then something buzzed angrily overhead and a full second later I heard the distant thud of a high-power rifle. Another bullet whined past our vehicle, only a few yards away, and again I detected the muffled thud of a rifle. Kangaroo poachers, of course! The mysterious, meandering light was their spotlight.

As long as they remained unaware of our presence, we were likely to collect a high-powered bullet! Shoving Mare out to lie on the ground, I dived into the Land-Rover's cabin, turned on the head-lights, and sounded the horn in several long blasts.

Another bullet came our way. Unfortunately our head-lights were pointed in the wrong direction, and slightly downhill into a clump of scrub. The horn, although it seemed loud, was apparently not loud enough. I dug out our trouble and camp light, which has a very long lead and plugs into the dashboard. We were certainly in trouble, so it seemed an appropriate action.

Then I flung the wire-caged light up into a mulga tree beside our vehicle, where I hoped it would be visible to the poachers. This had the desired effect. There were no more shots and that strange, meandering light vanished as mysteriously as it had appeared. The poachers probably thought they had stumbled on to a camp of Mount Wood station hands and beat a hasty and silent retreat. But just to be on the safe side, we dragged our Dunlopillo out on to the ground and slept there.

We don't often sleep on the ground because once, while camped along the Birdsville Track with drover Len Cant, we came close to being overrun by a minor "rush" of cattle in the night. The nights had been hot, so we made up our bed on the ground about 50 feet away from the Land-Rover, but fortunately between two large boulders. During the night, some sort of a disturbance started a rush and for once I was a bit slow in waking up. By then it was too late to dash for the safety of the Land-Rover.

We just stayed put while cattle thundered past all round us. Those two boulders, less than a yard high, probably saved us. In avoiding them, the stampeding cattle also avoided us. So far as I can recall, those few noisy, earth-shaking minutes represent one of the few times I have been really scared in the Australian bush.

Dingoes are the hardest of all wild animals to photograph in the Outback. Good shots of them in their native habitat are rare. It's a fair bet that any close-up of a dingo you have seen was taken of a tame pet or in a zoo. You can be lucky, of course, and sight one within camera range when you stick your nose out of the tent in the morning. That is, provided you are camped in remote country. But don't count on it.

A vehicle doesn't worry a dingo too much, while it is moving. But be ready to shoot your pictures the minute you stop, because once you halt, your quarry will remain still usually no more than thirty seconds—and then move steadily away. Following a dingo on foot is usually fruitless, unless you possess a very large tele-photo lens. Better to try again in the vehicle, or give up.

Of course, if you have suitable equipment, stalking any game is feasible, provided you have patience, plenty of time available, and some knowledge of bushcraft and your quarry's habits. Local knowledge is important, too, and it is always worth while obtaining information from local people on the whereabouts of the birds or animals you are seeking. They can often direct you to out-of-the-way waterholes or patches of green feed that you would never locate yourself. At such places, birds and animals congregate—and if the area is off the beaten track, your quarry may be much easier to approach than identical specimens along the more used roads or tracks.

Animals aren't stupid. They soon learn to associate man with danger. A kangaroo that lives beside the road near Bourke, New South Wales, is much harder to get

near than one out on lonely Cooper Creek.

If you are seriously interested in wildlife photography, here are some tips that might help you next time you undertake a camera safari:

Once you reach an area where you are likely to encounter suitable subjects for your camera, *always* have your camera close at hand and ready to use.

By ready to use, I mean fitted with the biggest telephoto lens you have, loaded with the correct film, and with the shutter speed and diaphragm opening set correctly for the prevailing light conditions. If clouds suddenly decrease the intensity of the light, take a meter reading and reset your camera controls. Then if a kangaroo or dingo suddenly appears, all you have to do is pick up your camera, focus, and shoot.

The following technical advice is specifically for 35mm camera users, but the general principles apply to larger formats. Use a fine grain film, but develop it in a developer more vigorous than the one recommended by the manufacturer of the film. Telephoto pictures lack contrast (and therefore sharpness) if given standard development. My standard technique, for example, is to use Ilford Pan F film, rated at Weston 200, and develop it in Microphen for eight minutes. (The "correct" speed of this film is Weston 50 and the "correct" developer is Neofin Blue, for about six minutes.)

In my opinion, the best type of lens for wildlife photography is a zoom. I use a Nikon 200-600mm, but a smaller lens can be used. Zoom lenses are definitely not as sharp as fixed focus lenses, I admit, but they make up for this failing in versatility. A 500mm lens is fine when your quarry is a long way off, but often you will find that your bird or animal has suddenly appeared much closer than you expected and you are unable to fit it into the viewfinder!

When this happens with a zoom lens, you simply "send your subject away" by reducing the focal length of your lens. The zoom also allows you to take a variety of different pictures of your subject from the one vantage point. By using its largest focal length, you can get extreme close-ups, and then varying long shots to show the creature in its natural surroundings.

If you are using a fine grain film in conjunction with a lens of 300mm or larger, you definitely need a tripod for good work, because your shutter speeds will necessarily be down around 100th of a second. We all fluke good hand-held shots, I know, but this doesn't mean you don't need a tripod on most occasions. By using fast films, which permit higher shutter speeds, you can use even a 500mm lens hand-held— but these films are grainy and lack contrast. What you gain in shutter speed is more than lost through soft, mushy pictures.

The best tripod is the biggest, heaviest one you can afford. Light-weight metal tripods are next to useless in the bush, because even a light wind causes them to tremble. The slightest tripod tremble is disastrous to a picture being attempted through a 500mm lens! My choice of a tripod is the Sydney-made Miller Senior, which unfortunately costs nearly $200 and seems to weigh a ton when you carry it more than a few yards. But it's rock steady, even in a stiff breeze.

Most camera gear these days is embellished with a lot of bright chrome work.

On a sunny day, reflections from your camera or tripod telegraph your position to your keen-eyed quarry. I paint over any shiny sections of my equipment with black matte paint. A dark green might be even better.

When stalking wildlife with a camera mounted on a tripod, tie a leafy branch to one leg of the tripod. This breaks up your outline and provides good camouflage. I usually wear a pair of long-sleeved khaki overalls which I once attempted to dye green, with mottled but effective (camouflage-wise) results. A few dabs of aniseed essence on your clothing help to disguise human scent. Sandshoes or rubber-soled desert boots are the best footwear.

My golden rule for wildlife photography is: get a picture at the first opportunity. This way you always bring back *some* record of your efforts. A picture of a bird or animal that is perhaps a little too far away is better than no picture at all. With this picture under your belt, you can then try to get closer. The comforting knowledge that you have at least one picture makes you less inclined to hurry things and perhaps startle your quarry.

If you finish up close enough to photograph your quarry's eyelashes, well and good. But this should be your last photo, not your first. The fellow who is satisfied with nothing less than a head-and-shoulders portrait of a dingo usually gets nothing, or has to go to the zoo for his pictures.

There is a wide variety of good equip-ment for wildlife photography on the market. I am strictly a 35mm man, due to the fact that my experience with larger formats has always been disastrous. My

own gear is exclusively Nikon, with the exception of the tripod. Needless to say, my cameras are all of the single lens reflex type. Range-finder cameras are not suitable for wildlife photography.

Some single lens reflex cameras, including the Nikon, have a split image focusing device in the viewing system. This should be discarded in favour of plain ground glass screens, particularly for long telephoto work. The cost of the changeover is only a few dollars. If you are buying a new camera, you can have plain ground glass in the viewing system at no extra cost.

Other makes of camera will no doubt do as good a job as the Nikon, and most of them are cheaper. I can think of two makes that are dearer, and in my opinion this additional expense is not justified. If your funds are low, Asahi Pentax gear is good, but unfortunately the lenses are of the screw mount type instead of the much faster bayonet type.

I would advise anyone who thinks he is interested in wildlife photography to start off close to home with the minimum of equipment. This would mean a camera fitted with a 200mm lens. Thus armed, the enthusiast need go no further than the outer suburbs of his native city to stalk such creatures as kookaburras, magpies, currawongs, seagulls, lizards, and perhaps some myxo-resistant rabbits. It takes quite a lot of patience and skill to get really good studies of creatures like these. More patience and skill than you may possess.

If you are still interested in wildlife photography after several week-ends of magpie or seagull stalking, you can go a bit further afield in search of more exotic subjects. The week-end driver cameraman from Melbourne can hunt lyrebirds and deer in the Dandenong Ranges or koalas in Gippsland. Sydneysiders can stalk deer in the Royal National Park or wallabies in the Blue Mountains. Equally interesting subjects are available in the environs of Brisbane, Adelaide, and other big cities.

A few camp-out week-ends spent trying to get pictures of wallabies, deer, a wedge-tailed eagle, or similarly elusive subjects will soon indicate whether you are really interested in wildlife photography and have the necessary skill and patience for it. If your interest remains keen and you obtain some successful pictures, then you can confidently begin saving for a tele-photo-zoom lens, tripod, and perhaps even a motor drive. Ultimately, you may find (as I did) that you need a four-wheel-drive vehicle to get to the places you wish to visit.

There is no doubt that the further from civilization you go, the better chance you have of getting really exciting wildlife pictures. A kangaroo in the middle west of New South Wales, which has probably been frightened by gunfire on a number of occasions, is much harder to photograph than a kangaroo out on the lonely Birdsville Track.

But you don't have to travel immense distances to find wildlife havens. By exploring quiet side tracks off the main roads you will often locate pockets of wilderness that are a wildlife photographer's dream come true. Such places may be within 100 miles of a capital city.

For kangaroos, dingoes, crocodiles, wild buffalo, and other large game you have to travel long distances. This applies also to birds such as emus, brolgas, plain turkeys, pied geese, jabiru birds, and wedge-tailed eagles. Until you can afford the time and the equipment to hunt such creatures, don't overlook smaller game much closer to home. Aided by a slip-on proxar (close-up) lens, a keen wildlife photographer can keep pretty busy in his own backyard, recording the wonderful world of insects.

Take it from me, a good picture of a white moth on a cabbage leaf is just as hard to get as a herd of buffalo in Arnhem Land.

There are plenty of other subjects for your camera in the Outback, apart from birds and animals. Some drovers and other outback characters are as shy as the most difficult wildlife, but not all of them. There's a lot of pleasure and satisfaction in getting a really good portrait or action shot of a bush man or woman—black, white, yellow, or brown. I'm even prepared to admit that there is some outback scenery worth photographing, provided the light is right and at least one human figure can be included, to provide a scale.

You can do quite well with the popular fixed lens type of camera that most tourists use to take slides for the benefit of the folks back home. The ideal thing, however, is to own a good quality 35mm camera, three bayonet-fitting lenses, and a good robust exposure meter. You should have a wide-angle lens with a focal length of 28mm to 35mm, a standard lens of 50mm to 55mm, and a medium telephoto of 80mm to 105mm.

This is my own *basic* equipment, although I have several camera bodies so that I can shoot colour or black and white at will.

If you cannot afford two camera bodies, you must choose to shoot either all black and white or all colour. It is usually disastrous to try both, because you will always seem to have colour in the camera when you want black and white, and vice versa.

Once again, a slow, fine grain film such as Ilford Pan F is the best choice for an all round film. For colour, although it isn't perhaps the truest, nothing can beat Kodachrome 11 for brilliance, sharpness, and reliability. Kodak process this film and their processing is remarkably good and reliable. If there is anything wrong with your Kodachromes, it is almost certainly your fault. If you expose the film according to the instructions in the packet and they are uniformly over or under exposed, this means the shutter of your camera is wrong. Most of them are, so unless the error is really bad, just use a faster or slower shutter speed until you find one that gives you consistently good results.

Don't go on a long trip until you can produce satisfactory colour slides or negatives. I've met scores of people in places like Alice Springs with cameras they had bought the day before they left home and still didn't know how to work. Their chances of getting any reasonable photos were small, because very likely their camera shutters were either fast or slow. It usually takes a few rolls of film to work out the correct method of exposure in any particular camera, so those unhappy tourists would very likely be home again before they managed a good picture!

Whether your chief interest is scenic or human, the basic golden rule of outdoor photography is: always have your camera ready. This may seem obvious enough, but it's amazing how many people leave their camera in the car when they get out to look at the view or talk with a drover in his roadside camp. By the time they realize there is something worth photographing, it is too far to walk back to the car, clouds have reduced the light, or the drover has jumped into the saddle and cantered away.

Having your camera ready means having it and your exposure meter hanging around your neck, with any additional lenses handy in your pockets, together with another roll of film. It is a bad mistake to get out of the car with a camera that has only a couple of exposures left on the roll of film in it. The leather strap attached to the camera is supposed to go over your head around your neck, so that your camera hangs suspended against your chest, fairly high up. Many people seem to think it looks silly to have a camera round their necks, but they look much sillier carrying a valuable camera dangling from its neck strap, bashing against their legs or the ground.

Most amateurs use slow shutter speeds, which result in fuzzy, unsharp pictures. The solution is simple; use faster shutter speeds. Unless you have an exceptionally steady hand, always shoot at 250th of a second and set your aperture (diaphragm opening) accordingly. Sometimes, with colour, you may be forced to use 125th or 100th of a second—but you should never come slower until you run out of apertures, or make use of a tripod. I shoot 99 per cent of my black-and-white photos at 250th of a second and most of my colour shots at 125th.

In addition to using impossibly slow shutter speeds like 50th or even 25th of a second, most amateurs make doubly certain of ruining their pictures by keeping well away from whatever they are photographing. The solution, once again, is simple; get closer. Each time you look through the viewfinder, ask yourself "What am I photographing?" If it is a man or a horse, then fill the viewfinder with the man or the horse. If it is a man or a horse against an interesting background, then fill the viewfinder with the man or horse and the interesting background. Blank sky or a corrugated iron wall are not interesting backgrounds.

As you look through the viewfinder, imagine you are looking at a finished print or projected colour slide taken by someone else. Then you will quickly detect the faults of your composition and make adjustments accordingly—usually by getting closer.

When you can't get closer to your subject, remember your telephoto lens. And remember that people and animals, particularly horses, look odd when photographed with a wide-angle lens, acceptable through a normal lens, and "right" through a medium telephoto of 80mm to 105mm.

By and large, the best outdoor lighting for scenes or human interest photos is side lighting or backlighting. This means that the sun is to your right or left, or directly in front of you. Put another way—early morning or late afternoon, for both black and white or colour. This is the exact opposite of what it says on the packet of your film, but it is nevertheless true. You should have a lens hood for each of your lenses, to keep out unwanted reflections, but never be afraid to shoot directly into the sun if the picture looks good to you.

For any picture, take a careful meter reading by pointing the meter at what you are photographing. If you are photographing the earth, point your meter

at the earth. If you are photographing a horse or a man or a tree, point your meter at the horse or the man or the tree—and make sure you are within 3 or 4 feet of the subject. When taking a general scene, point your meter slightly down. Most amateurs tend to read the sky with their meter, which means that everything except the sky in their picture will be under-exposed. Of course, if you are photographing clouds or a sunset, or a mountain range or a string of camels silhouetted against the sky, *then* you read the sky. But only then.

The Outback is a dusty place, so you

should have a skylight filter permanently screwed on to the front of each of your lenses. This will keep grit off the coated lens surfaces and you can safely use a handkerchief or the cuff of your shirt to wipe dust off the filter—which will stand years of this treatment and cost only $3 or $4 when it eventually needs replacing. A skylight filter makes no difference to your exposure of colour or black and white.

If you are interested in people as subjects, don't try to pose them. Just ask them do they mind if you take a few photos, then follow them about and shoot them in action as the opportunity presents itself. The trick here is to anticipate what is about to happen and try to get yourself in the right place for the potential picture. For example, if your drover has the billy on the fire and is digging in his tea bag, get yourself on the other side of the fire, take a meter reading, focus up—and you are all set to record a picture of him tossing a handful of tea into the bubbling billy. For portraits, don't ask him to pose, but wait until he is talking to one of his mates, or rolling a cigarette, then use your 80mm or 105mm lens for a few candid shots from a range of about 8 feet. One of them should be good provided you take a careful meter reading and shoot at 250th of a second.

Don't make the mistake of using your wide-angle lens on people or animals, unless you are specially after weird and wonderful effects. Used close-up, such lenses cause wild distortions—which can be used to good effect by professionals, but are *you* a professional? On the other hand, if you photograph people or animals with a wide-angle lens from a distance of more than 10 feet, they appear insignificant.

So the moral is: if you want to fit some people into your picture, use your standard (50mm or 55mm) lens and stand further back.

When you do use your wide-angle lens, for scenic and general shots, make sure there is plenty of interesting material close up in the foreground—trees, fence posts, the corner of a building, a vehicle, or interesting ground features such as red sand, gibbers, or lush grass. Who ever wrote the classic bit on the film packets about always remembering to "frame" your picture with trees and suchlike probably had wide-angle shots in mind. Don't have too much sky in a wide-angle picture. When in doubt, point your camera down to include uninteresting foreground rather than interesting sky. Better still, go and find some interesting foreground before you shoot.

Whatever lens you use, the way to get really good pictures is to take as many as you can possibly afford. Professionals do this. Don't be satisfied with your first photo of anything. There is always a better one to be taken. So, if the light gets better or the action improves or moves to a better location, take another shot of the same scene or the same drover. And if things suddenly begin to look even better, take a third picture, and a fourth. . . .

This can become expensive with colour film, and is a good argument in favour of using black-and-white materials. Or you can become very selective in your subject matter and instead of shooting everything in sight, save your ammunition for occasional fusillades at really good subjects. When you can school yourself to do this, you will be on the way to good pictures.

Anyone with a genuine love of the outdoors, or a strong interest in wildlife or scenic photography, eventually has to come to grips with camping. I use this term deliberately, because although life under canvas can be idyllic, and is usually portrayed thus in books and magazines, it can be hell if your planning and technique are astray.

A carefree life under canvas is only possible if you are properly equipped and have at least a smattering of bushlore. It should be understood at this stage that camping to me means getting away from it all and living in harmony with nature in a secluded location far from the maddening crowd. I do not mean crowded resort tent-slumming at holiday time.

The camp-ground camper is satisfied with what he calls a change from his normal environment. He is happy merely to be somewhere else and finds novelty enough in continuing his normal daily routine under canvas. He enjoys a bit of fresh air and blue sky and the pretence of going back to nature, but he prefers to share the adventure with his fellow man. He does not give up any home comforts. In many popular country and seaside resorts, canvas towns spring up, where tent guy ropes intermingle and the atmosphere is that of Saturday morning in the suburbs. In these crowded, insanitary, fly-ridden tent slums, nothing further from going-back-to-nature could be imagined.

I don't know why people scurry from the ugliness and regimentation of suburbia to the ugliness and regimentation of camp-ground life. Perhaps it is because city living today breeds in many people a vague but gnawing dissatisfaction with their way of life. But its comforts and the soporific glow of T.V. dulls the initiative of all but the most vigorous. Frustrated city dwellers rarely fight free of their suburban bondage and blaze new trails. Even during their few weeks of annual freedom they are too dispirited to do more than simply follow the mob to one resort or another, even if they don't like the place much.

They have been conditioned all their lives to put up with what appears to be the inescapable frustrations of life and so, like Shakespeare's Hamlet, they prefer to ". . . rather bear those ills we have, than fly to others that we know not of."

The camper who raises his tent in splendid isolation reaps a harvest of almost indefinable pleasures.

Genuine outdoor lovers face a big problem during the holiday period if they aren't prepared to camp anywhere except right beside their motor-car. Nowadays everyone has a vehicle and there are few back roads that aren't frequently explored by fugitive campers in search of peace and solitude. This year's delightful, isolated hideaway may be dotted with a score of tents when you return next holiday.

Bushwalkers have no problems in this respect. With all they need on their backs, they just walk over the next hill to peace and privacy. Some determined away-from-it-all campers are beginning to turn to four-wheel-drive vehicles in order to set up their tents in isolation. A Land-Rover (or Jeep) certainly allows you to push further into the wilderness, but it is a luxury hardly to be considered by the average once or twice a year camper.

A cheaper, temporary solution may be to invest a few shillings in the 1964 series of military survey maps of your favourite camping districts. The scale of these comparatively new maps is about an inch to the mile. They show many roads, tracks, creeks, and farm buildings not marked on tourist maps. They are a genuine guide to adventure for those who prefer to escape from the company of their fellow man while camping. The maps cost about 50 cents each and are sold by people like Robinsons and Gregorys in the capital cities.

By carefully studying these maps, you can plan a quiet camping holiday in secluded, unspoilt bushland sometimes only a few miles from overcrowded camping resorts. For a few years, at least, they should allow anyone who really wants to camp in solitude to do so. After that, at the present rate of "progress," even the loneliest bush tracks will be crowded with cars, and tents.

The most satisfactory solution, of course, is to avoid the holiday rush periods when you go camping. During the cooler months, the roads are comparatively free of traffic and there is little competition for camp sites. There are other advantages to camping in the off-season: there are few flies and mosquitoes, ants are less active, and because of the cooler weather, food keeps better and things like butter don't melt.

Go-it-alone campers, particularly those who are new to blazing their own trails, should travel light. They should remember that the basis of camping is living a simple life close to nature. Many campers make hard work of their holiday by going over-equipped. Their hoped-for simple existence becomes hopelessly complicated with cumbersome gadgetry.

Remember that if you are exploring new side roads and tracks, you can't be very adventurous if you are towing a large

trailer or if your car is so heavily laden that it tends to sink into the earth and bog the minute you leave the bitumen or gravel road. If you know exactly where you are going, trailers are fine, but if you want to go exploring, leave them home.

The average size family sedan is big enough to accommodate two adults and two or three children and everything they need for a fortnight's camp. A station wagon has room to spare. To save space, dispense with all non-essential gear such as folding stretchers, stoves and lamps, saucepans, collapsible washbasin stands, collapsible metal fireplaces, ice-boxes, portable folding toilets, and suchlike.

Instead of stretchers and conventional mattresses, take inflatable mattresses; instead of gas, petrol, or kerosene stoves, take a box of matches and a wire shelf out of a discarded refrigerator (for a cooking grid); instead of a pressure lamp, take a car battery trouble-lamp with a long lead; instead of saucepans, take pack-inside-each-other billycans (easy to lift off the fire with a stick and less likely to be tipped over because they have no jutting handles); instead of the other items mentioned— simply don't bother.

Your tent is the most important item of camp equipment. Hire one if you don't go camping very often. You can do this in most capital and large cities. If you buy one, get the best you can afford. (Many excellent tents are sold secondhand for about half their cost new, having been used only once or twice.)

For family camping, the auto-tent is ideal because it has full standing room inside. Get one from an old-established maker, with roped edges and walls that can be raised individually in hot weather.

Buy two extra poles so you can "abdul" (raise) the front wall of the tent to make a shaded eating area. If they don't come with the tent, have weighted netting walls made for the three sides of this front "porch," to keep out insects. You will need extra guy ropes and tent pegs for your front porch.

The metal pegs for your guy ropes, by the way, should be at least 15 inches long and as thick as your little finger. Don't economize and buy light ones. You should need an axe to drive them in (and hook them out).

Cooking gear should be kept to a minimum, say four or five nesting billycans and a long-handled frying pan. Tin plates are best because they stand up to rough usage and can be placed on hot ashes to keep toast or a meal warm. Tin or enamel mugs are best, for similar reasons. If you like stews, or have an ambition to "wallop up a damper in the dark," an iron camp or Bedourie oven is handy. Two plastic wash-up dishes, with broad bases and straight sides (so they don't tip up easily), are essential—one for the dishes and the other for toilet use.

As you have dispensed with your ice-box (useless off the beaten track), you need to stock foods that keep. Plenty of different types of salami, and similar, cheese, eggs in cartons, tinned tomatoes, beetroot and (dill) cucumbers, long-keeping continental style breads, potatoes, onions, carrots, cucumbers, tomatoes, oranges, apples, plus whatever tinned foods take your fancy.

Milk? Use powdered milk or do without. Butter? This will keep longer than you think without an ice-box in hot weather,

or no grass underneath. You can spot such places a mile off. Unless a lot of other campers have been there before you, there will be plenty of dry wood underfoot in such stands of virgin country. This will include dry leaves and twigs, plus sticks and boughs as thick as your leg.

Provided there is water within half a mile, set up your camp near such a place and you will have no firewood worries. It is much easier to break up dry sticks and limbs than it is to chop them, by the way. Not on your knee, but under your boot. Hold one end of any stick up to an inch thick in one hand and let the other end rest on the ground. Now step on the stick a bit nearer the ground than the middle, pull up, and it will break. Thicker sticks should be leant against a log and jumped on. You can also break quite large dry boughs by bashing them against standing trees or over logs. But make sure the point of impact is more than half the length of the bough from you or your arms will take a bad jolt.

Boughs too thick to break can be laid across the fire so they burn through and then the two halves placed on the flames. Chopping dry wood with an axe is the last card in the pack for most veteran campers. Axes are strictly for driving in tent pegs or cutting green stakes to strengthen your table.

Which brings up an interesting point. Very heavy, large, and expensive folding tables are often sold to campers. You can save weight, space, and money by using instead a flimsy card table which you can buy at any secondhand shop for a few shillings. They are light and unstable, but this is easily fixed. Simply drive in a long stake beside each leg and then lash the table legs to the stakes with heavy cord.

When you cut young saplings for any reason, take the trouble to walk into the bush some distance before bringing your axe into use. In this way you will prevent the roadside and your campsite from being slowly denuded of trees.

If you find an ideal location for your camp and intend staying there for at least a week, it is worth spending some time over your choice of a tent site.

Ideally, it should be on ground that will not receive any water from the surrounding countryside if it rains. Shallow drains should be dug along the walls of the tent, to lead away any water coming down from the roof or from surrounding ground. Place the earth from these drains against the walls of the tent and then lift the bottom of each wall and peg it down *outside* the long mounds of earth. This will prevent rain beating against the side of your tent from finding its way inside. Instead, it will go straight into your drains.

A small flat-topped mound is the ideal site for your tent, but you will be lucky to find such a perfect situation. Try to position your tent so it is shaded from about midday on. It is all right to put your tent near or under a smallish green tree, but don't camp under very large trees. There may be a big dead bough hidden up among the foliage just waiting to crash down on you.

Ants in the sugar and jam? Keep sweet things in jars standing in old tins half filled with water. Don't forget your motorcar as a place to store foodstuffs and other gear. Parked in the shade, with the doors propped open, it will keep fairly cool and remain ant proof. Leftovers going bad in the heat? Curry those uneaten sausages and stews. Use the new imported pastes rather than the powdered varieties we all know so well. With no other substitute save curry herbs, several hundred million Indians still get along without refrigeration.

Rubbish? Bury this regularly. It is all right to distribute a few apple cores, crusts, and carrot scrapings about the surrounding bush for the wild creatures. But remember that kitchen refuse will soon attract additional flies to your camp. Empty tins can be placed on the fire at night, jumped on, and buried with the bottles next morning. (The heat hastens the rusting process; the jumping on is fun and reduces their bulk.)

Burn all your paper and cardboard rubbish on the campfire. When you walk through the bush, don't mark your route with a trail of empty cigarette packs, silverfoil wrappings, and lolly boxes. It's no trouble to return empty packages to your pocket and drop them in your campfire when you return. If you *must* unload them immediately, step off the trail, kick a hole in the earth beneath a bush and scuff them over with a layer of dirt and leaves so they will mould away to nothing out of sight.

If you cannot demonstrate your appreciation of the virgin, unspoilt wilderness that has given you refuge, you should stay in an organized camping ground where a man is paid to pick up your rubbish.

Maintaining and storing food supplies and meal preparation seem to be the biggest stumbling blocks for many campers. The chief trouble is that some people don't seem able to change their eating habits when on holiday. Once it is accepted that you don't *have* to eat weeties and milk as a prelude to breakfast, and have a roast with all the trimmings on Saturday, the problem dissolves.

Breakfast? Eggs, fried, poached, boiled, scrambled, omeletted, with toast and marmalade; or bacon and toast sandwiches, or tomatoes and sausages with toast, and so on. Lunch? Sandwiches every time, or curried leftovers. Dinner? Tinned or pressed meats or salami, garnished with sliced tomatoes and onions, or potato salad and suchlike.

Meals like these free the cook for most of the day, and make washing up a simple, quick task. (Take along a couple of plastic-coated dish racks and leave plates, cups, and cutlery in them until next mealtime.) If you can't do without multi-course meals for a few weeks each year, maybe you should stay home, or book in to a guest house or rent a cottage with proper kitchen facilities. Cooking on a campfire is an art, but it is not a difficult art to master. The first and most important step is to build and light your fire well before you want to start cooking. This is because you are supposed to do your cooking on or in red hot coals, not leaping, blazing flames. A good bed of coals on which to cook a family meal takes about half an hour to form.

The wire ice-chest shelf (mentioned earlier) thrown on to the coals makes a good level platform on which to stand frying pan or billies, and it can be used as a toast rack. You can make toast six or eight pieces at a time on this wire tray while the bacon and eggs keep hot in the frying pan. Boiling the tea billy can be done in the flames of the fire soon after you light it, but don't bother suspending it on sticks

or hanging it from tripod contraptions. Just kick down a "nest" among the burning sticks with the heel of your boot and place the billy there. When it boils, lift it off with a stick slipped under the handle, remove the lid (using a handkerchief if you have tender fingers), hold the billy on the stick back over the flames until it bubbles again—then toss in rather less tea than you would use for the same quantity of water at home.

If you don't like smoky tea, keep the lid on your billy. The idea that a stick balanced across the top of an open billy will keep out smoke is a lot of eyewash.

Stew is rightly among the most popular bush meals. It can be made in endless variety in the camp oven, and the surplus can be curried for safe carrying and a change of diet next day. Many popular city dishes are basically stews, which can all be made over a campfire. These include: ragout, pilau, goulash, and various spaghetti sauces.

Brown the meat with onion or garlic and whatever spices are needed, add water, and simmer with any other ingredients required. Mixed spices, bay leaf, chilli powder, curry paste, plenty of onions, and garlic, plus a few small cans of tomato *purée* are all you need for "Continental" camp cooking.

For example, "bouillabaisse" is only a sort of fish soup, which is easily made in a large billy or the camp oven. Any sizeable saltwater or inland river fish is suitable. Remove all bones and simmer with carrots and onions in powdered milk mixture (if fresh isn't available), adding a lump of butter and light sprinkle of sugar during cooking. Easy?

For damper, the basic mixture is one large cup of self-raising flour, plus a generous pinch of salt and a scant quarter cup of water (just enough to bind the dough into a rubbery mass). Any size damper can be made to this formula. For a small camp oven, use four cups of flour, a scant cup of water, etc. (Caution: Too much water means a leathery damper.)

During cooking, the dough increases in volume by one-third to one-half, depending on the temperature of baking. If your coals are too hot, the outside of the damper will be burnt and the inside raw. Insufficient heat produces a flat, rubbery mess.

After placing your dough in the camp oven (greased), dig a foot-deep hole near your fire and place in it two shovelfuls of coals and white ash. Place the camp oven in the hole and cover with two more shovelfuls of coals and ash, slightly more if necessary, to cover the oven (top and sides) completely. Allow forty minutes maximum cooking time. If unsatisfactory, try again. Your third or fourth damper will be excellent. Damper does not keep well and should be eaten on the same day or the next day at latest.

Add a walnut of butter or clean dripping and a teaspoonful of powdered milk per cup of flour and you have a more palatable scone loaf. (Rub the butter into the dry ingredients.)

For a Johnny cake, another bush favourite, to each cup of flour add two teaspoons of sugar and one-third of a cup of raisins or mixed fruit.

When you get sick of damper, scone loaf, and Johnny cake, try "puftalooners," as they are called in the bush. Get some deep clean fat bubbling in the camp oven and into it drop spoonfuls of the damper or scone loaf dough. Leave the lid off and remove the puftalooners when they are golden on all sides. Drain off fat on paper and roll in sugar if you have a sweet tooth.

The best meat for bush cooking is the meat you buy in the town butcher's shop. There is a lot of nonsense published about bush cooking by people with strong imaginations, strong teeth, and no tastebuds. Rabbits and wild duck are delicious, but don't waste time chasing goannas, pythons, wood grubs, or kangaroos. (Any part of the kangaroo is edible, of course, if you are hungry; but there is nothing special about the tail—the best meat, for stewing, with plenty of tasty spices, is from the fleshy haunches.) Wild pigs are often diseased and should be avoided.

If you are going on a long camping trip, remember that fruit is usually dear and often hard to get in many country areas, particularly inland. On your way out of the city it may be worth while to buy a small case of apples or oranges at a roadside stall —or one of each if your family likes fruit.

Good substitutes for fresh fruit are small cans of juice to which vitamin C is added during processing. Buy them cheaply at home before you leave. Keep flies away from your fresh meat by tying it up in sugar bags. Oh, and one other thing.

Don't forget the matches!

If you have to camp in a camping ground, a stove of some sort is necessary, as wood is invariably non-existent in such places. Here I'm all for the latest innovation: gas cooking. The rechargeable gas cylinder devices are excellent indoors and have few drawbacks.

Gas lamps are excellent, too—but if price is a problem, don't forget the trouble-light from your car battery. Take the car for a run every second day if you use the lamp for more than four hours each night.

Next to gas burners come petrol stoves and lamps, with kerosene-fuelled appliances a very bad last. The trouble with these old faithfuls is that kerosene around a camp always seems to taint food sooner or later. Also, the appliances have to be primed with methylated spirits, which is a nuisance and means you have to store two kinds of fuel. (Petrol appliances are not in the least dangerous, by the way, despite what some people think; but petrol stored in a bottle inside your tent or car can be a hazard, because of the possibility of breakage.)

Camp-grounds in summer usually have a big population of flies, attracted to the overflowing garbage drums and primitive

toilets. Insect curtains on your tent are doubly important. Although they don't usually get much publicity, there are occasional outbreaks of dysentery in crowded camping grounds each summer. So have your flyspray ready for any of these pests that manage to penetrate into your tent. And don't eat out of doors.

At night, insects can be troublesome, even if your netting curtains keep out the flies during daylight. This is because of the fanatical devotion all sorts of flying bugs have to light. They will crawl in through tent eyelets and push under the walls to reach it.

You can save yourself a lot of trouble by hanging your lamp *outside* the netting in such a position that enough illumination falls inside to eat or read by. If you must have your lamp inside the tent, the worst place for it is directly above the table. From this position it will send down a constant rain of incinerated bugs into the jam and salad.

If you transport your camping gear in a trailer and there is no space problem, folding camp stretchers may be preferable to inflatable mattresses. They are handy to sit on and you can store suitcases and other gear under them. But if you are going to have stretchers, tables, and chairs in your tent, don't buy one with a canvas floor. The legs of your furniture will soon punch and tear holes in this covering. A few yard-wide strips of canvas between beds is a good idea, though, if you don't like carrying sand or dirt into your bed each night.

Your tent, by the way, if transport offers no problems, should be the largest you can afford. A big tent with $200 worth of camping gear inside it is a much more comfortable place to live in than a small tent with $200 worth of gear crammed into it.

It should be possible to raise any wall quickly and easily to catch the breeze on a hot day or night—and there should be an insect curtain handy to hang in this space.

When erecting the tent, rope each wall individually to corner poles. Then, if you want to raise a wall later on, you can do so without having to re-tie the adjoining wall. Don't forget to have extra poles and pegs to abdul these walls.

Beachside campers may do well to have even larger pegs than those already recommended. Home-made wooden pegs will hold better in sandy soil than even the largest iron pegs. Make them at least two feet long. There is nothing quite so uncomfortable and embarrassing as having your tent blow away during a sudden wind squall.

One last piece of advice: there is really no sense in trying to keep up with the Joneses when camping. By trying to look neat and clean at all times, you will saddle yourself with extensive wardrobes of clothes, bulging suitcases, folding ironing boards, petrol irons, coat-hangers, and racks—and poor old mum will be condemned to daily queueing at the communal laundry and an endless round of scrubbing and mixing liquid starch.

You will have brought down on your family all the cares and restrictions of suburban drudgery. This is the wearisome grind you are trying to escape by having a camping holiday. So take your oldest clothes, and few at that, a pair of thongs or sandshoes, a battered hat—and enjoy yourself.

If you are interested in outdoor photography or simply in roaming out of doors, sooner or later you will want to press farther afield than you have previously. The idea of a Grand Tour, lasting perhaps several months, may present itself.

Five recent graves along the Birdsville Track emphasize that Australian outback motoring is still fraught with peril. The graves were dug for an English migrant couple and their three young sons who suffered the awful penalty of death by thirst, because their vehicle ran out of petrol one Christmas between Marree in South Australia and Birdsville, just over the border in Queensland.

Hundreds of inland tourists by car court disaster each year and only luck saves them from the fate which befell the English family. Thousands more push their luck along the presumably safe, bitumen-surfaced Stuart and Barkly Highways in the Northern Territory. They are blissfully unaware that a comparatively minor mechanical failure can force them to abandon their vehicle to rust by the roadside, or lead to severe physical hardship, perhaps death, if they attempt to walk to an off-the-road station homestead for help.

A few touring, outback motorists die or narrowly escape death each year and anyone planning an inland motor tour should bear in mind that death is a constant backseat driver on the roads and tracks of the Never-Never country.

You can learn from the mistakes of others. It is a harsh thing to say, but the dead Englishman who lies buried beneath the sandhills flanking the Birdsville Track, provided a classic example of what not to do.

These were his mistakes. He attempted a very tough journey in the worst month of the year—December. He told no one that he was leaving Marree and, therefore, nobody knew where he was going or when he expected to arrive. He was not expected anywhere and, therefore, was not missed.

He travelled in an unsuitable vehicle for a novice, outback driver in unknown sandy country—a heavy sedan of conventional two-wheel-drive. He decreased his chances of getting through by carrying three passengers and all their luggage. He further decreased his chances by hauling a trailer behind his vehicle.

He failed to ask for advice on the condition of the track before setting out. Tracks like the Birdsville change their course from month to month, depending on the movement of sandhills, local rains which flood claypans, and so on. It is almost impossible for strangers to find their way along such routes without first-hand and very up-to-date advice.

He did not carry enough water. A safe minimum in this sort of country is a gallon a day per person, with an extra gallon per person for every third day. He did not carry enough petrol. It is sound practice in the back-o'-beyond country to have enough petrol to take you "there and back" to the presumed next source of supply.

A vehicle leaving Marree for Birdsville (325 miles) which does 25 miles per gallon should, therefore, carry about 26 gallons of petrol. This may seem ridiculous to city drivers, but it is good sense in the bush. A flood in the Diamantina may turn the northbound traveller back on his tracks to Marree, when he is within a stone's throw of Birdsville. Or he may be blocked by sand, or simply bushed in the last 100 miles and have to retreat along his tracks back to Marree. Or he may take a few wrong tracks for 30 or 40 miles and back while trying to pick the right track to Birdsville. Finally, it is a fact that a normal mileage per gallon of 25 can be cut back to 16 on a soft, sandy track.

After breaking down on the track, the Englishman failed to stay with or near his vehicle, which was found within two days. After finding water near by, he left it and the car to attempt the impossible—a walk through unknown country to an uncertain destination in fierce mid-summer temperatures.

The Englishman may have made other errors of judgement, but those listed were more than sufficient to bring disaster to the entire family.

If you are intending to be an outback motor tourist, here is some advice on the subject gleaned during twelve years and 250,000 miles of far-outback driving. Remember it well. It could save your life.

Do not go unless your car is in tip-top condition. Other people have gone around Australia in bombs, but this does not prove you can. Scores of abandoned cars along far-outback tracks and highways show that many ill-prepared cars did not make it.

Do not go unless your tyres and tubes have travelled less than 15,000 miles. Recaps are unreliable under arduous conditions.

Do not go until a qualified motor engineer and a qualified car electrician have okayed your vehicle. If they say the vehicle needs money spent on it, stay home if you can't afford to have the work done.

If your radiator has not been overhauled during the previous two years, take it to a specialist and ask him to dismantle it completely, clean it, reassemble it, and fit new hose connections top and bottom. This costs about $10.

Do not go without a workshop manual and a spare-parts manual for your make

of car. Even if you are not mechanically minded, they may help some better qualified traveller to get you out of trouble along the track. A country garageman who has never seen your make of car before, can probably fix it if you supply him with a workshop manual. The spare-parts manual is equally important when replacements have to be ordered from the nearest capital city by telephone or telegram.

Spare parts for Holden, Volkswagen, and Ford are obtainable in most country centres, but replacements for other makes invariably have to be sent away for. This takes many days.

Do not go unless you carry at least the following spare parts: fanbelt; top and bottom radiator hoses with clips; set of distributor points; condenser; coil; spark plugs; carburettor repair kit; water pump repair kit; an inner and an outer wheel bearing for a front and a back wheel (if they are not interchangeable) complete with rubber oil seals; wind-screen wiper blade; headlight globe; assorted lengths of light and heavy wire, rubber or plastic hose, electrical wiring, and several dog-clips, split pins, and nuts and bolts, as well as insulating tape.

Do not go unless you carry adequate tools with which to replace all the parts mentioned and to replace a wheel or mend a puncture. A good mechanical jack is essential. In fact, two mechanical jacks are often required for bush repair jobs. You can buy two for the price of one hydraulic jack.

Optional spare parts include: a mainleaf with rubber bushes already fitted; two shackle bolts; one front and one rear axle (if not interchangeable), with inner and outer bearing for both (if not interchange-

able); a light hand-winch for pulling your vehicle out of a bog.

Learn to do the following jobs on *your* car (and acquire the necessary tools): dismantle and reassemble the carburettor; change and reset the distributor points; replace the fanbelt; replace a shock absorber; change a wheel; adjust the brake shoes; bleed air from both the clutch and brake hydraulic systems; adjust the clutch pedal free-play; replace an inner wheel bearing; replace a headlight globe; start the vehicle without the aid of the ignition key.

None of these things is really difficult, but they are fiddlesome jobs to do, particularly under bush conditions, if you haven't done them before—or don't have the right tools. A good bush driver can usually replace a broken spring, a wheel bearing, or an axle.

Do not go in the November-to-February summer period.

Do not go without sufficient petrol, water, and engine oil. Plan always to obtain petrol and water only at towns. It is inconsiderate in the extreme to expect homesteads to supply you. They may be down to their last few gallons of petrol until the next truck gets through and down to their last few rungs in the rainwater tank.

Buy at least six $4\frac{1}{2}$-gallon jerricans for your trip. They cost only $1 each and are the best possible type of containers for knock-about bush work. Use four for petrol and two for water. In addition to petrol and water, carry an oil change for your engine, just in case you crack the sump on a boulder.

Never go on a bush track for any distance without inquiring locally about its con-dition. With few exceptions, all outback roads shown on the map are bush tracks. This practice serves many purposes. It saves a lot of time and trouble if the track is closed by sand or flood, it enables you to find your way along the track (which may divide several times without signposts between you and your destination), and it lets local residents know that you are travelling in the area.

If you don't turn up at the next homestead, someone may come looking for you within a couple of days.

In really tough areas, advise the local policeman, if there is one, of your plans. He will probably suggest that you call in at a homestead somewhere near the other end of the track, and let them know you got through. When he is on the air (radio) during the next few days, the policeman will receive word that you passed, or failed to do so.

Provided you follow this procedure, a breakdown in even the worst desert country should not mean anything worse than a wait beside your car for two or three days. By this time you will have been missed and someone will come looking for you.

But remember, outback policemen and settlers have other things to do apart from risking their lives searching for lost or broken-down motor tourists. You are without question a nuisance and a humbug if people have to rescue you in the Outback, so take all the care humanly possible to see that you do not break down or get lost.

Whenever you leave a town, homestead, creek, tank, fence or cross a side road, note your speedo reading in a notebook. Then you will at least know how far it is back to where you've been, should things go wrong.

When you see tracks joining the one you are on from an acute angle behind you, pull up about 20 yards beyond the point where they meet your track and look *back* at them. Should you have to return over your track for any reason, you won't mistakenly follow any of these offshoots. In your notebook record the mileage, with the words "FALSE left (or right) lead if returning."

Always keep a close check on how much petrol you have left. Then, if you suspect you have taken a wrong turn somewhere, you can turn back to your last refuelling place before you reach the point-of-no-return. Aided by your record of any possible false leads, you shouldn't make any mistakes getting *back* to your last refuelling point.

You will often mistakenly take side tracks instead of the main track, because they seem better used. There is no way of avoiding this at times. After 5, 10, or perhaps 30 miles you find yourself at a bore that has obviously been recently repaired, or a newly built stockyard, or an oil rig (hence all the fresh wheel marks that fooled you). So you just about-face and return to the main track and continue on. This is why you have to carry plenty of petrol in the Outback. It may be only 100 miles to the next refuelling point, but a few false leads can easily double your mileage.

If you do break down or get lost in difficult, strange country, stay near your vehicle. This is absolutely the number one rule for survival. An aeroplane, a keen-eyed stockman, or a policeman or a black-tracker can find a motor-car much more easily than a wandering, aimless human.

Furthermore, you will survive longer near your vehicle because you will have aboard several jerricans full of water, plus an additional gallon or so in the radiator and engine block, if things get desperate.

Even if you know or suspect you have broken down off the main track and fear that no one will ever find you, stay near your vehicle. No matter what remote, unfrequented locality you have chosen to lose yourself in, there is every possibility that within four or five days a boundary rider, a stockman, a drover, or professional shooter, will turn up.

If you are tempted to leave your vehicle, remember this: you can't carry more than 2 gallons of water any distance and will probably drink the last drop in your second day of weary plodding. In your car you should have 6 to 12 gallons, enough for a fortnight if necessary. The moral is: stay near your vehicle.

Of course, if you have been following a well-defined track and know with certainty from your speedometer mileage that a homestead is only 10 miles behind you, and if the weather is cool, it may be safe to try to walk back. Don't walk in the heat of the day. Start very early in the morning, preferably before sun-up, if it is a short walk. For a longer walk (maximum should be 20 miles), start late in the afternoon. This will give you several hours' walking before dark. Then you can go on at first light of the cool of the next morning.

If you start at daylight and fail to reach your destination by 9 or 10 that morning, rest under a shady bush until late afternoon, and continue then (or return to your car if the exertion seems to be knocking you up). Don't try to walk with more than 2 gallons of water, as the added weight will quickly tire you.

When you do leave your car to walk back to a homestead you have passed, leave a note on your vehicle saying when you left and your intended destination.

Don't change your mind and follow side tracks in the hope they will lead you to a homestead closer than the one you know exists because you have previously driven past it. Pay no attention to printed maps, which may show stations which are now only ruins, or indicate that stations are right on the main track, when in reality they are miles off on a faintly marked set of wheeltracks.

Because of this last fact, never set out to walk ahead to a station marked on your map. Attempt to walk to places you know exist because you have been past them. If in doubt, stay near your vehicle.

If you have reason to believe that a search may be in progress for you (because you have notified various reliable people of your intended destination and time of arrival), and if you suspect you are not on the main track, a ground sign for searching aircraft should be made. The capital letter F indicates that you require food and water; an X announces that you are unable to proceed but implies that you have sufficient food and water. There are other code letters but the F or X signs are the only ones likely to be used by the average broken-down or lost motorist. Make the letters on a flat, clear area within 100 yards of your vehicle.

Clothing and bedding stretched out and held on the ground by rocks can be used to make a letter, preferably about 10 feet long. Suitcases, jerricans, spare wheels, and other gear can also be called into service.

If you are waiting beside your vehicle because you are broken down or hopelessly lost, do not stray beyond sight of your car unless you have a good sense of direction, or a compass, or both. On the flat, featureless plains or in sandhill country, where you are most likely to be lost, finding your way is far more difficult than in rugged country where there are plenty of landmarks.

A non-bushman who wanders a few hundred yards out of sight of his vehicle may never find it again.

As a last word on being lost or broken down in bad country: *don't panic.*

If, after a day or so of waiting, you are beginning to plan an attempt to walk overland to some uncertain destination, you are about to panic. The idleness of waiting leads to excessive worrying, which leads to panic. So keep busy by tinkering with your vehicle, enlarging the size of your air-search ground sign, or building a pile of material that will make a smoky fire, should a plane appear. Whenever you start to think of walking away, say to yourself: "To leave my vehicle is to panic and to panic may be to die."

You don't have to attempt the Birdsville Track to get yourself into serious difficulties while motoring in inland Australia. Plenty of people cross the Nullarbor or follow the bitumen Stuart Highway from Alice Springs to Darwin, and the Barkly to Mount Isa, blissfully unaware that only luck is seeing them through. It is quite a simple matter to break down on any of these main highways and find that the nearest garage is more than 200 miles away. If you are not a competent mechanic, or do not have the required spare parts, this is what happens:

You wait, possibly twelve hours, for another vehicle to come along. The driver, another tourist, cannot help you, but agrees to take a message to a garage at Tennant Creek, or Camooweal, or Katherine. He arrives in town after the garages have closed, but stays overnight and delivers your message in the morning.

The garageman, quite reasonably, shrugs the matter off, saying: "He's probably fixed the trouble and got on his way by now. I've been caught like that before. You drive 200 miles to help a bloke and find he isn't there."

Your friend, having done his best, continues on his way. By lunchtime next day you are still beside your vehicle, waiting. Various motorists who have stopped have given advice about what they think the matter is, but the exact nature of your vehicle's ailment remains uncertain. Eventually you realize that you will have to get to a garage in person, if you want a mechanic to examine your car. You get a lift a few hours later and arrive in town well after dark, so all the garages are closed.

Next morning, after visiting several garages, you engage a tow-truck driven by a mechanic to drive the 200 miles to your car. The trouble turns out to be something that cannot be repaired by the roadside, and your vehicle is towed the 200 miles to town. If the mechanic diagnoses something seriously wrong with, say, your gearbox, the cost of the repair work and the tow may be over $300. (For Continental cars, it may even exceed that.)

The work may take a week, particularly if you have broken down on a Friday and if parts have to be flown from Adelaide or Brisbane. If you haven't got ready cash to

cover the cost of repairs, plus a week's hotel bill for you and your family, and if you are due back at work by a certain date, you are in serious trouble.

If your car is a bomb or worth only $500 or less, you may decide to abandon it by the roadside, thumb a ride to the nearest town, and fly home. If it is worth between $500 and $1,000, you may get the repairman to tow it to town where you can sell it (probably for only $500) and fly home.

If it is worth more than $1,000, the tow and repair work may be worthwhile. And if you haven't the cash, you can fly home, save it, and retrieve your vehicle some months later.

But let us assume your car is a recent model. You arrive in town just at closing time and it is a case of first thing in the morning. But with other work on hand, your vehicle may not get attention until lunchtime, or even later. Once the offending section of your vehicle has been dismantled, it is pounds to peanuts that replacements will not be available, unless the car is one of the makes already mentioned.

Sometime that afternoon a message is sent off to Adelaide or Brisbane, ordering the parts. At best, it will be one day, and possibly two or three days, before the parts arrive by plane.

Then the job has to be done. And you have to pay up in cash. In addition to this amount, which will be anything from $50 to $300, you will have a hotel bill and the cost of the tow to meet.

The actual trouble that put you off the road may have been something as simple as a collapsed wheel bearing, worth only a few dollars, but the whole episode will have cost you something like $200, plus a full week of worry and frustration. If a week-end intervenes, or the wrong parts are forwarded from the capital city, or something like a gearbox has to be repaired, ten days to a fortnight can slip by.

This frightening little story is in no way exaggerated, so do not undertake a trip from Alice Springs to Darwin as if it were an extended Sunday drive. Make sure your car is in first-class order, take plenty of spare parts and tools, and carry plenty of petrol and water. You can get just as thirsty beside a bitumen road as you can in the Birdsville sandhills.

A shortage of water on a main highway can lead to death, if the rules of outback behaviour are broken. Unless you can actually see a homestead or a windmill, do not wander into the scrub or along any side tracks in the hope that they will lead to a home or tank. A city man can easily get hopelessly bushed only a few hundred yards off the Barkly or Stuart Highways.

The same golden rule applies, no matter where you are when you break down in the far Outback: *stay near your vehicle*. And do not forget that radiator water. It may sound like a poor sort of drink as you read this, but if you are ever really thirsty, it will taste like nectar.

Some forty years ago, the Member for the Northern Territory was found unconscious beside his motor-bike in central Australia, his mouth choked with oil from the bike's sump.

The moral of this whole story is: do not undertake far-outback motor-touring lightly. If you do, your holiday may turn into a horrible nightmare from which there may be no awakening.